INTROSPECTIONS ON *The Gita*

The central philosophy of the Gita teaches us how to face a catastrophic situation in life with equanimity and courage and a stable and settled mind.

INTROSPECTIONS ON
The Gita

NARAYAN SINGH MASUDA

edited by

INDRAJIT SINGH RATHORE

New Age Books

Introspections on The Gita

ISBN: 978-81-7822-392-6

First Indian Edition: Delhi, 2012

Published by
NEW AGE BOOKS
A-44 Naraina Industrial Area, Phase-I
New Delhi (India)-110 028
Email: nab@newagebooksindia.com
Website: www.newagebooksindia.com

Printed in India
at Shri Jainendra Press
A-44 Naraina Phase-I, New Delhi-110 028

Rao Narayan Singh Masuda

Rani Kamala Devi

To the memory of my father whose presence
awakened and stirred my spirit
and my mother whose absence aroused
a perennial and unrequited love,
together becoming an inspiration for this book

Indrajit Singh Rathore

MESSAGE

The Gita along with the Bible and Quran, is one of the three most widely circulated religious texts in the world. In India, particularly the Gita has had a profound influence on succeeding generations down to the present day. Profound commentaries on it have been written by numerous scholars all the way from Adi Shankracharya to the great commentaries of the 20th century including Lokmanya Bal Gangadhar Tilak, Sri Aurobindo's classic work, Shri Krishnaprem and many others.

By its very nature the Gita is so rich that it lends itself to endless interpretations based on each writer's individual consciousness. Rao Narayan Singh Masuda who I knew for many decades as a mature and intelligent person, a man who was in politics and yet above it, has also written his own thoughts on the Gita. I recall that whenever we met, we often discussed the Upanishads, the Gita and other spiritual texts. Fortunately he entrusted his hand written manuscript to his grand daughter and these have now been edited by his son Indrajit Singh Rathore to make them available to a wider reading public.

I am happy that this interesting and thought-provoking commentary on the Gita is now in the public domain, and I hope it will be widely appreciated.

1 January 2012 — Karan Singh

Dr. Karan Singh
Member of Parliament
(Rajya Sabha)

CONTENTS

Message vii

Acknowledgements xi

Editor's Foreword xiii

Preface xvii

1. Arjun's Despondency 1
2. The Destructible Body And The Indestructible Soul 7
3. Action And Inaction 15
4. Divine Incarnation-Avatar 21
5. Divinity Within & Unity In Diversity 27
6. Sanyasi - The True Yogi 35
7. God And Nature 41
8. Cosmology Of The Spirit 45
9. A Remarkable Tolerance Towards Diverse Paths Of Worship 49
10. The Glorious Attributes Of God 55
11. Vision Of The Cosmic Form 59
12. Worshipping The Manifest And The Unmanifest & The Ideal Man 69
13. The Field And The Knower Of The Field 75
14. The Three Natural Traits 81
15. The Tree Of Life 87
16. Divine And Demonic Natures 91
17. The Faithful And The Misguided 95
18. The Final Word 99

Major Themes With Textual References 109

Index 123

ACKNOWLEDGEMENTS

I am deeply grateful

to my daughter Meera for so carefully preserving the manuscript of the book which my father entrusted to her;

to my wife Amrita for urging me to have it published;

to my sister Vijaylakshmi, my daughter Meera and my son Parthsarthi who generously assured me that they would share costs if they arose;

to late Kripal Singh Shekhawat, Padma Shri, who painted the magnificent painting of Krishna and Arjun on the chariot, engaged in dialogue, before the battle at Kurukshetra - which he was kind enough to allow me to acquire and which adorns the front jacket of the book;

to Durgesh Nandini, my cousin, for painting the ' Virat' or cosmic vision of God which Arjun had the privilege to witness and which is on the back cover of the book;

to Faith Singh, the charismatic and ingenious founder of the Jaipur Virasat Foundation and inspiration behind the Jaipur Festivals, which ultimately spawned the Jaipur Literature festival - for encouraging me with the book and introducing me to Namita Gokhale, author and Director of the Jaipur Literature Festival;

to Namita Gokhale for finding time to go through the manuscript and being encouraging and complimentary;

to J.P. Jain of Motilal Banarsidass Publishers for his interest;

to Rajeev Jain and Jyotsna Khandelwal of New Age Books for her patience, kindness and valuable guidance and for accepting the book for publication;

Without them the publication of this book would only have remained a dream.

INDRAJIT SINGH RATHORE

EDITOR'S FOREWORD

My father had entrusted a hand-written manuscript of his 'Introspections on the Gita' to my daughter when he accompanied her back from Woodstock School Mussoorie, saying ' in your hands this is not likely to get lost!' He was right. Many years after his passing away she found it while unpacking after a transfer and handed it over to me urging that I edit it and have it published as was his wish.

Throughout his life when I had a chance to be with him he would inevitably launch into philosophical discussions on the amazing spectrum of Indian thought, culture and civilization, illustrating with vivid accounts from the myths and Puranas[1]. My earliest childhood memories are of quiet enjoyable evenings in his prayer room before a splendid silver idol of lord Vishnu[2] almost two feet tall and exquisitely sculpted. There he would read passages from the Tulsi Ramayan[3] about the marriage of Lord Shiva[4] and Parvati[5] with great zest and vigour, bringing to life the ascetic bridegroom and his unlikely retinue. I would long for evening to arrive so we could resume the stories he would recount with the incense wafting and the wicker lamps casting their magical light, as his sonorous voice boomed theatrically.

My father was a real 'Karma Yogi'[6] throughout his chequered life as a Raja, a politician, a mystic and a philosopher. He survived numerous calamities, traumas and upheavals of circumstances but with faith and equanimity soldiered on. In his youth he lost the guiding hand of a dynamic father, having lost a mother in infancy. Suddenly he found himself saddled with overwhelming

1 Ancient Hindu legends and myths.

2 Second god of Hindu triad: the preserving, sustaining and restoring power.

3 The Ramayana epic by 16th/17th century philosopher- saint Tulsi Das.

4 Third deity of the Hindu triad: the annihilating and dissolving power.

5 Lord Shiv'a consort.

6 Man of righteous action.

responsibilities of the kind most of us would quake to bear. Six younger brothers and two sisters to educate, marry and settle though he was still in his teens himself. Suddenly his hopes of pursuing higher education under the umbrella of a strong and wise parent were shattered.

When he married somewhat unconventionally, the most beautiful woman the land had possibly produced, his life acquired a new meaning and was filled with new-found happiness, helping him to bear the awesome responsibilities towards his siblings. But life delivered yet another cruel blow and in less than a decade she succumbed to the scourge of the times, tuberculosis - a slow and harrowing ailment which compounded the tragedy of inevitable death, ironically on the eve of the invention of streptomycin. He was devastated with the additional burden of having to handle the grief and trauma facing the three children she bore him. For some time he lost his balance. Later when he recovered he never forgot her and as we grew up were surrounded by her magnificent portraits and photographs everywhere we looked, never letting her memory pass away.

Later as a politician he came to be acclaimed as a 'Dev - Purush'[7] by one and all for his selfless services to the people, his childlike simplicity, uncommon compassion, humour and friendliness, loyalty and incorruptibility. Even today, decades after his active political life, scarcely a day passes when someone unknown, be it a fellow politician, clerk, civil servant, neighbour, academic or villager does not recount some anecdote about him when I happen to inform them that I am his son. I have yet to come across another politician being called 'Dev - Purush' and wonder sometimes whether it is only a cynical comment and a euphemism for someone naive and rather unworldly who didn't have a clue how to feather his own nest. Most however who call him that, surely mean it earnestly I would like to believe. He was gentle to a fault and we children were quite capable of bullying him. If we picked up something valuable and said we wanted to keep it, he just didn't know how to say no. When he passed away thousands upon

7 Saintly individual.

thousands of villagers from the region flocked to the funeral at our village - people on roof-tops, people jostling everywhere and as we carried him to the pyre, the villagers shouldered us out saying he was theirs.

Being mystical, he told me he had visions in his teens of a blue form in a white halo. The silver statue which he commissioned he said remarkably matched the form in the vision. The Gita was his constant companion and he found all answers he sought in facing the challenges of life within it. His love and devotion towards his 'Isht Dev', the form of God he cherished, was inspired by Arjun's[8] for Krishna[9]. He always spoke of Him as a friend and guide he could trust with utmost faith. God was both mentor and companion and he would sometimes talk of him in lighter vein as if pulling His leg.

Yet near the end that friendship faltered. When confined to the bed wracked by pain and unable to exercise control over bodily functions, in anger and frustration he said to me in a voice reduced to a whisper " there is no God". I knew from the look on his face that he was lying and like Arjun in pain and frustration he had cast away his bow. Later that evening sitting on the terrace we saw a bright shooting star traverse the sky. I knew then that he had left. Now his face had relaxed in sublime peace and like a distant dawn, a trace of a smile had appeared. In death at last his face was cast in faith.

While earlier he had published commentaries on the Upanishads and the Gita in chaste scholarly Hindi, together with some one-act- plays on characters in our epics, in his final years he sought to complete the manuscript on the Gita in English. The full weight of his varied and trying experiences, his knowledge and scholarship and his deep faith and love for God made him a worthy commentator on the Gita. His presentation is unique and makes easy reading. The introspections bring out the essence of each chapter lucidly and imaginatively. I have read several commentaries that are verbose, dialectic and pedantic which leave one exhausted,

8 Hero of the Mahabharat epic and protagonist of the Gita.
9 Divine incarnation of Lord Vishnu and protagonist of the Gita.

if not confused. But his presentation helps one to grasp the essence of the Gita with facility and enjoyment, enabling one to understand how its message may help in one's time of crisis.

Finally I must confess that I have been fairly liberal in the editing, filling gaps where they needed to be filled on the basis of his conversations with me, simplifying the language when it tended to get archaic and seeking to provide a sequence which would feel easier on the mind. My intention in this was to present the sum and substance of his introspections rather than a literal presentation. The language had to be modified to suit the requirements of present-day readership. The commentary is important for its content rather than a literal rendering. My editorial effort, I have no doubt, will facilitate a more lucid understanding of his introspections on the Gita.

Indrajit Singh Rathore

Jaipur
December 1, 2011

10 Mystical musings in the Vedas, Hindu scriptures.

PREFACE

My 'Introspections on the Gita' in English was written after my 'Gita Manan' * in Hindi which however only went up to the ninth discourse. According to some analysts the next nine chapters are basically a further elucidation of the central philosophy of the Gita, though in my view not entirely. The eleventh, for instance, portrays the Cosmic Self, conceived rather imaginatively, which dispels thoughts of a gory nihility after death and provides hope of the existence of a benign universal force. Likewise the thirteenth and fourteenth chapters dwell on the embodiment of the soul and its progress through many life times to ultimate liberation. Chapter twelve dwells on the advantage of worshipping a God with form as against worshipping Him as unmanifest and formless. Despite some repetition every chapter has something important to say.

Personally what inspires me most in the Gita is the urgings to Bhakti Yoga, the Yoga of utter faith and concentration. This is not to neglect the virtues of Gyan Yoga, Yoga of knowledge, equally important in discriminative concentration on the mysteries of life and ultimately Karma Yoga the path of action.

The central philosophy of the Gita teaches us how to face a catastrophic situation in life with equanimity and courage and a stable and settled mind. It helps us to develop a personality in the physical outer- self reflecting the perfect harmony of our innermost self, the soul or Atma; a personality that would make the outer-self completely conform to it, to be able to face the dire circumstances with wisdom and courage.

The Gita after thus preparing the individual allows him a glimpse of a cosmic being, one that is dynamic, life suffusing and eternally

*Manan means 'introspections' in Hindi.

energetic, reflected in our own timeless physical universe. The Cosmic being thus visualized is the source of all its fragmentations and the fragments therefore are imbued with all the qualities of the progenitor, however dormant. The Gita thus projects the fundamental Hindu beliefs of divinity within us and the ubiquitous presence of divinity in every being and atom of creation which is apparently divided but in essence united by transcendental divinity; unity in diversity. Western scholars have called this Transcendental Monism as contrasted with the Dualism of the Judaic faiths where the creator and his creation remain separate and distinct.

Thus the Gita urges its votaries to develop 'same-sightedness' (Sam-Darshinah) in recognition of the divinity both within and around us, in every category of person and being and even in inanimate nature. This is a call to treat every person with equal respect and compassion, a plea to extend such compassion to the animal world and beyond the animate to inanimate nature, matching our ecological concerns of today.

The Gita also propounds in chapter four the unique concept of Avatar; divinity incarnate on the material plane. Not only do souls as fragments of divinity reincarnate time and again on account of their acquired Karmic compulsions but the supreme Godhead itself reincarnates, though in His case voluntarily, from age to age to correct the errors that develop in His atrophying creation, as Avatar.

In chapter seven and nine the Gita emerges as the epitome of tolerance towards diverse faiths and beliefs emphasizing the need to allow different categories of people to worship in the manner they please undeterred, for " whatever divine form any devotee with faith wishes to worship, the same faith in him I make unwavering."

The Gita also speaks in detail about our corporeal self and the Self within it. This deepest Self is described as the Karta or innermost dynamic of the field of our corporeality. The Gita defines and develops the concept of the soul and the manner of its transmigration and rebirth. It speaks of the importance of engaging in righteous action for purification of the personality to eventually match the perfection of the soul that inhabits it and rejects obsessive ritualism and the misconceived abandonment of action and temporal duty through reclusive asceticism as false renunciation and hypocritical inaction. It stresses that the altruistic ideal of dispassionate and selfless action is the single most important goal of life, leading to liberation.

The central purpose of the Gita is to enjoin one to realize one's true nature 'Svabhava', the Self within; which once grasped would create an intuitive intelligence in every performance of worldly actions.

The dialogues in the Gita are divided into eighteen chapters, each called Yoga. The first is called Arjun Vishad Yoga; Arjun's despondency. The next is called Sankya Yoga and so on. The word Yoga suffixed to each title can be loosely interpreted as Science. Thus Karma Yoga would imply the science of action, Dhyan Yoga, the science of meditation etc.

As the Gita is not a treatise or commentary, we cannot expect a logical and evolutionary flow of ideas. The discourse being in the form of a dialogue, several issues recur from chapter to chapter as they are re-emphasized. While certain themes dominate the dialogues in a chapter, they are not presented exclusively. Thus there is a free flow of ideas with considerable repetition, back and forth in the presentation and the given title of a chapter does not encompass them all. In the interests of clarity and to enable a proper grasping of the essence of the message I have sought to present the essential themes emerging in each chapter in some logical sequence together with an analysis based on my introspections and I have given the chapters my own titles to highlight the most important theme of a chapter.

To illustrate the central message and context of each chapter I have also selected several key verses and placed them immediately after the chapter, this time with the original title in Sanskrit for the chapter from which the excerpts have been taken. A mere commentary and analysis would become academic and tiresome. It is like writing endlessly about a person without ever showing his photograph. The original verse, even in translation carries its own force and gives one a feel of the original message which then makes the commentary more legitimate. I have also given a synopsis before each chapter listing the important issues discussed in it.

Finally at the end of the book, after the eighteenth chapter, I have highlighted what I believe are the major themes and unique features of the Gita. Here again I have painstakingly selected a collection of verses which together go to support my presumption regarding the substance of a theme and placed them immediately after that theme, something like a reference to context. The reader after reading the verses would have the conviction that what is being claimed about the theme is indeed so.

I do hope that all these aids to understanding will help the reader to grasp the essence of the Gita. It would be useful to have a copy of the Gita's translation at hand, so that after reading the commentary the reader can refer directly to the entire text of the verses relevant to the chapter thus enabling him to understand its full import. At the end, I have no doubt that the whole process will have a transforming effect on the reader.

NARAYAN SINGH MASUDA

CHAPTER

1

ARJUN'S DESPONDENCY

The Bible of India - A dialogue not a sermon - Gita an episode in the epic Mahabharat - The backdrop of battle between the Kauravas and Pandavas - Arjun's despondency - Making a virtue of a weakness - Self-deception - Allegorical implications - The dialogues relayed by Sanjay clairvoyantly to the blind king Dhritarashtra.

The Gita is well qualified to be called the Bible of Hinduism. Bible should mean here a scripture which provides the very principles on which life is to be led for a people in search of a viable spiritual and moral foundation serving as a guide.

Unlike other world scriptures, the Gita does not become a law - giver. It is in the form of a discourse like many other Indian scriptural writings but more so it is a lecture given on the spot urging one to perform one's duty when confronted by a difficult dilemma. No pretexts are allowed to shield behind custom, convention or tribal loyalties, no opportunity allowed to indulge in pious resignation or renunciation to escape the harsh circumstances, no easy escape permitted from shouldering your responsibilities.

The dialogues between Arjun and Krishna constituting the eighteen chapters of the Gita occur in the great Hindu epic the Mahabharat, in the 'Book of Bhishma[11]'. The Gita's seven hundred verses are only a brief episode in the epic's over hundred thousand verses but represent the synthesis of Hindu philosophy and beliefs.

11 Bhishma Pitamaha, the celibate hero of the epic Mahabharat and grandsire of the warring cousins the Pandavas and the Kauravas

The scene opens with the Kaurava and Pandava cousins readying for war at the battlefield of Kurukshetra over disputed succession for the Kingdom of Hastinapur. Arjun the most chivalrous and heroic Pandava asks his charioteer Krishna to steer the chariot between the opposing armies to enable him to assess the strength and morale of his opponents. The lone chariot winds its way to the centre of the battlefield as conches blow, horses neigh restlessly, armour and weapons clink, banners flutter atop magnificent chariots and the sky turns a furious orange ready for the fateful battle. Here seeing his numerous peers, teachers, grandsires and kinsmen arrayed in battle against him, he is suddenly smitten with deep remorse and overwhelming sorrow. Either a surreptitious fear of defeat creeps into his marrows or an altruistic realization of the perils of annihilation of the family and clan. These mixed feelings he garbs in noble ideals of loyalty to clan, the immorality of extermination of family and the crime of hostility towards friends and peers and sermonizes that with decline of family, time honoured customs would perish, leading to impiety and decent to hell. He argues that if the adversarial kin have clouded judgment, on account of greed and feel no guilt in the immorality of engaging in the extermination of family, it is no reason for their side to pursue similar sin and to fail to see reason by engaging in such an unrighteous war. Right from the twenty ninth verse to the end of the first chapter Arjun's despondency, doubt, confusion and prevarication become compounded till he casts away his bow in utter dejection asserting that he will not fight.

Arjun's pious realizations if anything have come too late. Confronted by fears and doubts, his faint-heartedness at the possibility of losing much if not all, now masquerading as honourable reservations, was clearly a form of self-deception.

Krishna, his mentor, seeks to attack this mentality of self-deception and as a friend and guide reprimands him in the ensuing chapter urging him to overcome his faint-heartedness.

Here let us pause to consider the impression that may be created on the superficial, lay reader by Krishna urging Arjun to fight. He may well wonder whether the Hindu Bible is actually a call to be warlike, urging its followers to acts of heinous aggression even against one's brethren! Therefore, not to be thoroughly misled, it is important to recognize its highly evolved allegorical connotations.

This is not about war at all though in the immediate context and setting it appears to be so. The armies arrayed on either side are the furious circumstances of life. The adversarial clansmen are the challenges in life demanding performance of ones duty. Arjun is the mind and ego of an individual confronting them. His faint heartedness and confusion are the reactions of the individual facing catastrophe. The chariot is his body and Krishna the charioteer is his soul and conscience, the indweller guiding him along the right path of action through intuitive understanding. As Avatar, friend and companion he is the soul but as the Universal Essence he is also the Super- Soul. The thinking functions are the bridle, the senses are the horses. The impending war is merely the field of action. It need not be a war; it could be any issue confronting an individual, demanding action. The refusal to fight is a refusal to act and Krishna urging him to 'fight' is no more than urging an individual to face any circumstances with responsibility and courage and engage in righteous action.

The events transpiring on the battlefield of Kurukshetra are narrated to the blind king Dhritarashtra, father of the Kaurava brothers and uncle to the Pandavas, by his clairvoyant courtier Sanjay in the secure confines of the palace. Being blind he is unable to be present at the battle as he obviously cannot fight. He is blind not merely physically but also metaphorically. He is reluctant to redress the injustice of denying the Pandavas their legitimate succession to his throne or even a share of the kingdom, out of unreasoning and doting love for his arrogant and evil first born Duryodhan whose sole ambition is to usurp that right and deny the Pandavas any compensation. This indeed is the reason for the ensuing battle. Meanwhile he perseveres in his hypocritical charade of equal love and concern for the Pandavas. He is convinced that the righteous Pandavas will be victorious in battle, particularly as they have the support of Lord Krishna and for this reason his concern for the fate of his wayward son Duryodhan becomes more acute. The dialogues of the Gita as we get to read them are thus the clairvoyant courtier Sanjay's narration of events to the blind king Dhritarashtra, as they occur. The fact that the dialogues, epitome of wisdom and ethical conduct, are being narrated to one who is cynical and has lost all sense of judgment and fair play is suitably ironical.

ARJUN VISHAD YOGA
(Excerpts)

Arjun said:
Seeing these my kinsmen, collected here prompted by war, my limbs fail me, O Krishna, and my mouth is parched up.
CH 1.28

My body quivers and my hair stand on end. The bow Gandiva slips from my hand and my skin burns all over.
CH 1.29

I am unable to stand; my mind whirls as it were; and Keshava[12], I see adverse omens.
CH 1.30

I do not foresee any good ensuing from the slaughter of kinsmen in battle. O Krishna, I hanker not for victory or empire or pleasures even.
CH 1.31

Of what avail to us is kingdom or enjoyment or even life, O Govinda[13]?
CH 1.32

Though myself slain by them, I would not, O Madhusudan[14], seek to slay them even for the sake of domination over the three worlds, how then for the earth?
CH 1.35

Although these, with understanding clouded by greed, see no guilt in the extermination of a family, no crime in hostility to friends, why should we not learn to recoil from such a sin, O Janardana[15], we who see evil in the destruction of a family?
CH 1.38 - 39

---

12 One who has wonderful hair, Krishna.
13 One who knows the mind of people, Krishna.
14 Slayer of the demon Madhu, Krishna.
15 One who helps people, Krishna.

Goaded by the greed of pleasures of a kingdom, we are, alas bent on perpetrating the great sin of killing our kinsmen.
CH 1.45

Should the sons of Dhratarashtra with weapons in hand slay me, unresisting and unarmed in the battle, that would indeed be better for me.
CH 1.46

CHAPTER

2

THE DESTRUCTIBLE BODY AND THE INDESTRUCTIBLE SOUL

Krishna tackles Arjun's self-deception psychologically, philosophically and metaphysically - Arjun's despondency used as a vehicle to disseminate veritable truths - Truths presented only in the context of facing life's challenges - The eternal soul and the perishable body - 'Atma' and 'Pran', the eternal soul and the subtle body - The gross and subtle sheaths enveloping the soul - Modern scientific analogies - 'Nishkam Karma', the central theory of undifferentiated action - State of enlightened bliss.

Krishna's reprimand at first seeks to tackle Arjun psychologically, shaming him for being unmanly, faint-hearted and feeble before proceeding to address larger philosophical issues which become the substance of the discourse.

It is interesting that the vehicle for presenting veritable truths in the Gita is Arjun's despondency. This is achieved through a dialogue between God incarnate and his human disciple. Krishna his mentor and charioteer seeks to overcome Arjun's reluctance to act in the performance of his duty and moral obligation, in the present case to fight a righteous war against his immoral kinsmen representing the forces of evil.

We need to note that the veritable truths are not presented in isolation or without context. The extraordinary revelation in chapter two about the true essence of man, the inhabiting soul and its nature are made only incidentally in the context of Arjun's refusal to act, so as to dispel his cowardliness and to put him on the path of rightful action. While the truth is indeed important and needs to be disseminated, this is not achieved through an academic sermon, rather it gets to be known in the context of Arjun's moral crisis, indirectly. For that reason the truth is more readily assimilated as a factor which helps in resolving human dilemmas and strengthening resolve in fearlessly performing ones obligations and duties. The secrets of the soul are not presented as nuggets of knowledge but rather as a panacea for what ails the human condition. Thus only does the discourse make the stunning revelations about the nature of the soul. It appears that the Gita has more concern for the human condition than interest in preaching veritable truths.

Without naming 'Atma', the soul, Krishna, with a trace of a smile as if to underline the foolishness of remorse, refers to the destructible body and the indestructible dweller within. Krishna explains that even if they do not die in a war, his adversaries will be overtaken by death some day, for death is certain for one who is born and rebirth is certain for one who dies, therefore there should be no cause for grief for the wise. In their origins beings are unmanifest, in their middle-state become manifest and then turn unmanifest again in the end but the in-dweller remains invulnerable, so why lament. The dweller within he explains experiences childhood, youth and old age in the body it inhabits. He explains further from where the dweller within comes and where to it finally returns. He also elucidates two factors which bring about these changes. One, the process that brings about childhood, youth and old age and another which brings the in-dweller from beyond and then returns it back to the beyond.

This in-dweller he says is indestructible, eternal, immovable, unmanifest, inconceivable and unchangeable. It is not scorchable by fire, impervious to water, neither getting wet nor drying, immune to heat and cold and incapable of being cut or wounded by weapons. It is neither born nor does it die, thus neither does it come into being, nor does it cease to be. It is unborn, inexhaustible, stable, all pervading, invulnerable, constant and ancient and therefore is not killed when the body is slain. It merely casts off a worn-out body and enters a new one; much like a man casting off worn-out garments dons new ones. This is perhaps the most remarkable, vivid, precise and beautiful description of the soul attempted in any religious literature.

Introspecting on the Gita one realizes that it refers to the soul as the indweller without initially calling it the 'Atma'. This is because it wishes to create an understanding of the concept in a novel way without relying on conventional nomenclature. In fact the Gita is a surreptitious revolt against age old ritualism and spiritualism of yore created by" Ved-vad-ratah" or dogmatic vedic orthodoxy which degenerated into elaborate and pedantic but ultimately empty ritualism.

The Gita later also refers on the one hand to a life force, Prana, that is the vessel of reincarnation and on the other to the individual soul, the 'Atma' , which it keeps calling the in-dweller. There are so many terms used to refer to the soul that at times one gets thoroughly confused. These are Atma, Purush, Jivatma, Prana, Jiva and Antaryami. After much introspection and research I would like to present the following explanations which would help in clarifying related concepts which figure again and again in the discourses.

The Jiva and Jivatma refer to the embodied Self, whereas the Atma refers to the divine essence not necessarily embodied. Purush often refers to the soul as the inhabiting 'person' which in that case is an embodied Atma. Antaryami means the one who dwells within and is often also a synonym for God in one's depths.

According to Indian philosophical traditions there are five layers which conceal the embodied inner essence. The first is the gross body which moves in a world of gross matter. The second is made up of the vital forces, 'Prana', the invisible life force which keeps us well coordinated when in good health and cheer. The third is the sheath of the mind and senses that drive the sense organs in the gross body. The fourth is the layer of understanding, 'Buddhi'. The last is the sheath of bliss, known as the causal body. The first is material and phenomenal while the others are spiritual or ethereal, called the subtle body. But despite being ethereal in some way they are substantial and capable of dissolution, unlike the 'Atma' which is indestructible.

The 'Atma' or Self is the in-dweller covered by these layers. With death the gross body disintegrates but the subtle body consisting of the other layers, leaves the sheath of the gross body and goes from birth to birth as the vessel of the incarnating entity. The nature of its new existence is determined by its 'Sanskaras' or inherited traits relying on past Karmas. Verse 8 Chapter 10 when it speaks of the soul taking the senses and the mind along at death, implies that the departing soul carries with it the subtle sheath of these acquired effects of Karma. The 'Sanskaras' are the permanent marks left by previous actions, inclinations, desires and acquired potential. While the subtle body is marked by all these traces and effects and 'odours', its in-dweller, the 'Atma' is not. The 'Atma' remains pure, eternal and uncontaminated, being a part of the Universal Essence, the 'Paramatma'. When liberation finally comes and the cycles of rebirth are terminated, not only the last gross body is shed but the vehicle for rebirth, the subtle body and causal body also disintegrate and the 'Atma' then freed from embodiment finally merges with the Universal Essence, the 'Paramatma'. An analogy often given in Indian lore is that the 'Atma' merges with Brahma even as drops of water in a collapsing wave merge with the ocean.

I felt that the above explanation of terms one frequently encounters in the Gita and an elaboration of the concept of reincarnation, though a bit detailed, was necessary for a clearer understanding of the essence of the Gita. Now for instance there would be no confusion when a reference is made to a life force, 'Pran', which becomes the vehicle for reincarnation as against the 'Atma'. The former is the subtle body the latter is the in-dweller, the former though ethereal is eventually perishable the latter is eternal.

Here, pondering the nature of the 'Atma', as defined by the Gita I could not help but wander into the realms of science and I hope to be forgiven for thus getting distracted. Indeed science too vouches that 'matter' is indestructible and nothing can totally cease to exist, it merely changes form. Science speaks of a 'Big Bang' in the cold dark primordial nothingness. Surely there was some hidden positive force in its dark bowels which sparked the explosion in the eternity of time and space and that spark with its chain reaction touched every atom of the universe. That spark was to my mind the great electro-magnetic point of creation and now it has spread to encompass every aspect of creation. It today embraces every facet of life, from genes to chromosomes to cells. Our life force reflects that spark within the complex of our corporeal cells held in harmony in the matrix of quantum reality of subtle waves binding the universe and upon death the parcel of impressions get carried forth in some subtle body to some other plane by the force of the particles that constitute the will and on the wings of a still subtler entity or complexity which we may call the soul-force of the 'Atma' into a new existence. Energy forming into matter and vice versa, dare I add, E=MC square?

Arjun having heard his charioteer's reprimand and words of wisdom gains a vision of an indestructible in-dweller and amazing spiritual insight, partially helping to overturn his state of mind, countering his corporeal attachments to the kinsmen arrayed in battle. From the Himalayan heights of metaphysics Krishna returns to the realms of psychology and ethics of life, preaching about doing ones righteous duty honourably lest one becomes an object of dishonour, slander and ridicule. He concludes, if one dies honourably in battle one gains the heavens and if one is victorious one gains mastery over earthly domains.

Krishna then propounds the Gita's central philosophy of temporal life, the call to perform ones duty selflessly and with the profound detachment of a Karma -Yogi, to whom no Karmic sin attaches. He speaks of the ideal of non attachment to the fruit of action, which is not to say having disinterest in ones goals or lack of spirit or energy in pursuing them. The action must be performed with total dedication and zest but one is not to be consumed with worry for the rewards nor when the results arrive be overwhelmed with joy at success or grief at failure. Having done ones best there has to be a detachment towards the results. Krishna emphasizes that one has a right only to action, that is to doing ones duty, not to the results. One must be even minded in success or failure for "wretched are the result seekers" and work done to perfection alone is 'Yoga'. Even mindedness extends to the 'pairs of opposites', to heat and cold, pleasure and pain etc. Such balance and resolve must go beyond ritualistic and scriptural obsessions for " to an enlightened Brahmin all the Vedas are as useful as a tank when there is a flood everywhere."

Arjun pointedly asks for a definition of such a man of steadfast wisdom, how does he speak, walk, what marks him out? Krishna replies that such a man is one who is absorbed in his inner self, without cravings, unperturbed, detached, unaffected by the vagaries of circumstances good or bad, in total command of his senses. Such a person is not a slave to his senses but moving tranquilly in a world full of sensual provocation is neither given to attraction nor aversion, his mind is discriminating and in a state of equilibrium. Such a person then is unaffected by sorrow and is at peace, having overcome longings and ultimately even the ego. He can truly be said to be in a state of 'Brahmi' or enlightened bliss.

SAMKYA YOGA
(Excerpts)

The Blessed Lord said:

Whence has this unmanly, heaven barring and shameful dejection come upon you, at this juncture O Arjun?

CH 2.2

Yield not, O Partha[16], to feebleness. It does not befit you. Cast off this petty faint-heartedness. Wake up, O vanquisher of foes!

CH 2.3

O Bharata[17], then smiling, as it were, Hrishikesha[18] spoke these words to the desponding one placed between the two armies.

CH 2.10

You grieve for those who should not be grieved for; yet you spell words of wisdom. The wise grieve neither for the living nor the dead

CH 2.11

16 Son of Pritha (another name of Kunti) - Arjun

17 Descendant of king Bharata, founder of the dynasty - Arjun.

18 Master of the senses - Krishna.

Nor I, nor you, nor any of these ruling princes was ever non-existent before; nor is it that we shall cease to be in the future.
CH 2. 12

As the indweller in the body experiences childhood, youth and old age in the body, he also passes on to another body. The serene one is not affected thereby.
CH 2.13

These bodies of the Indweller, who is eternal, indestructible and immeasurable, are said to have an end. Fight therefore, O Bharata.
CH 2.18

He who holds it as slayer and he who considers it as slain, both of them are ignorant. It slays not nor is it slain.
CH 2.19

It is neither born nor does it die. Coming into being and ceasing to be do not take place in it. Unborn, eternal, constant and ancient, it is not killed when the body is slain.
CH 2.20

As a man casting off worn out garments puts on new ones, so the embodied one, casting off worn out bodies enters into others that are new.
CH 2.22

Weapons do not cleave it, fire burns it not, wind dries it not.
It is uncleavable, incombustible and neither wetted nor dried. It is eternal, all pervading, stable, immovable and everlasting.
CH 2.23 / 24

It is unmanifest, unthinkable and immutable. Therefore knowing it as such, you should not grieve.
CH 2.25

Death is certain for that which is born; birth is certain of that which is dead. You should not therefore lament over the inevitable.
CH 2.27

Beings are all, O Bharata, unmanifested in their origin, manifested in their mid-state and unmanifested again in their end. What point then for anguish?
CH 2.28

Some look upon the Self as a marvel, as a marvel another speaks of it, and as a wonder another hears of it, but though all hear of it none knows it.
CH 2.29

But if you will not wage this righteous warfare, then forfeiting your own duty and honour, you will incur sin. People will ever recount your infamy. To the honourable, infamy is worse than death.
CH 2.33 / 34

You only have a right to your actions no claim to the fruits thereof; do not be moved by the fruits of action; nor be inclined to inaction.
CH 2.47

Motivated action is, O Dhananjaya[19], far inferior to that performed with equanimity of mind; take refuge in the evenness of the mind; wretched are the result seekers.
CH 2.49

The wise, imbued with evenness of mind, renouncing the fruits of their actions, freed from the fetters of births, verily go to the stainless state
CH 2.51

That man attains peace who lives devoid of longing, free from desires and without the feeling of 'I' and 'mine'. This, O Partha, is the state of abiding in Brahman, of absolute truth. Attaining this, none is deluded; if even only at his last hours he dwells in it he attains to oneness in Brahman.
CH 2.71 / 72

19 Winner of wealth - Arjun.

CHAPTER

3

ACTION AND INACTION

Arjun the mythical hero - A counterpoint who draws the truth from God incarnate - Contradiction between action and renunciation - Action is mandatory for the living - God too is perpetually active in creating and sustaining the world - But remains unattached - Ordinary people cannot be expected to engage in selfless action and should be left alone - However Arjun should engage in undifferentiated action through performing his duty in battle.

Arjun is much like a Hero from Greek mythology. Those familiar with the epic Mahabharat, of which the Gita is actually one chapter, know him to shine out as the archetype of the ideal Indian male. He is handsome beyond measure, generally shown bewhiskered, fair, athletic and tall. He is also the most proficient archer in the land, astute warrior, brave, courageous and fearless - none can match him in the field. He is also a devoted and beloved spouse of Krishna's cousin Draupadi, ideal brother and kinsman, faithful friend. His character is flawless and exemplary. He is righteous to an extreme and an introspective and questioning thinker. He is no dumb unquestioning disciple. Throughout the Gita, the 'celestial song' of God incarnate, he is the counterpoint that probes and evokes answers making them resonate like commandments about veritable truths. Without his incessant questioning the emerging truths would not have the lustre they acquire in counterpoise. He is never reticent, though sometimes bashful, in challenging his divine friend and mentor to clarify what he does not comprehend. He never meekly accepts an argument or explanation till it removes his doubt and dispels his confusion. Krishna loves him for these qualities and when he feels particularly endeared to him he refers to him as Partha.

In the ensuing chapter Arjun begins the dialogue by professing complete confusion over what has just been said. If the ideal is blissful equilibrium through self control and introspection, detachment and meditation, the path of knowledge, why then is he being asked to engage in the violent activity of warfare, full of wrath and destruction?

Krishna, the Guru, immediately counters that one cannot achieve perfection by mere renunciation or by abstaining from action become 'inactive'. Under the force of nature ('Gunas' or innate traits born of nature,'Prakriti') everyone is helplessly driven into activity. Even for survival the body itself is continuously in a state of motion. A person may delude himself that he is doing nothing, sitting inactively, while his mind is full of sensual thoughts. Such a person is a hypocrite. The ideal person is one who while being fully active, remains detached and in control. He asserts that action is therefore superior to inaction and that Arjun needs to act. Krishna points out thus that the very nature of life of a living being cannot be bereft of action or thought.

The Gita provided new meaning to concepts occurring in the old scriptural literature. Scriptural phraseology which with the passage of time had become anachronistic and misleading was presented anew. For instance in 'Sankhya' philosophy, Prakriti or nature implied complete cohesion of all organs and elements (i.e. the body and its environs) with absolute composure and peace of mind. Such a state automatically would lead to inaction and disinterest in everything. But nobody not even a recluse can remain without action. Organic necessities like eating or answering calls of nature impel action. Within the body the heart and digestive systems etc all engage in action. Existence therefore requires action.

Speaking of the inevitability of action Krishna traces the origins of action to the Gods and Demy-gods. He refers to the creative principle Brahma (calling him Prajapati), who created mankind in the beginning, urging it to propagate and engage in ritual sacrifices of 'Yagya' which would fulfill their needs and desires. Annie Besant the famous theologian translated Prajapati as the 'lord of emanation' who initiates action and discharges the natural law through the action of the 'shining ones' the Devas (divine forces) by ushering in the seasons and the cycles of nature. Thus action or Karma triggers the process from high or low. Man should engage in the selfless action of 'Yagya' which does not mean mere ritual sacrificial prayers or making offerings to the gods for personal gratification but work performed with the right frame of mind which is the true 'Yagya'. Thus the ideal is to perform ones obligatory duty.

Krishna then confesses that He is Himself perpetually engaged in action which should be an example to be followed by all. Unique and beautiful insights suddenly appear in verses 22 and 23 revealing to us the nature of the Godhead. Krishna explains that there is nothing which he cannot achieve, being omnipotent and yet He remains incessantly active, for were he to cease such activity not only would he set an example of indolence for mankind but the physical universe would annihilate. What is important is to actually sustain the universe and be a supreme example for the multitude to emulate. Thus the creation and sustenance of the universe through his intense activity and engagement, are His obligatory duty which He selflessly performs, though he need not as he is not required to achieve anything. The supreme example of selfless undifferentiated action has been set through the extraordinary discharge of the responsibility of creation and this example Krishna wants mankind and in the instant case Arjun to be inspired to follow.

Yet he admits that such a supreme ideal cannot immediately be imposed on the ordinary person who is a slave to his physical impulses which he calls the 'Gunas of Prakriti'. One could say that the Gunas are the combination of inherent traits and attributes imparted by nature or Prakriti to a given object or person to enable it to react to stimuli. Thus given their inherent traits the majority of beings would remain attached to serving their selfish needs and desires. Krishna urges that such mediocre beings should be left alone and not unsettled with lofty goals beyond their comprehension. It is enough that they are engaged in action to meet their obligations. Such beings should be gently guided to higher ideals but not forced to act against their basic constituent nature.

Finally Krishna asks Arjun to slay the enemy within - the insatiable fire of desire and attendant wrath which dominate the body, the senses, the mind and the intellect, thereby veiling the wisdom of the Atma and destroying knowledge and discretion. He asks Arjun to turn his thoughts inward, surrendering his actions to the Lord, overcoming his fevered mental state and engaging in dispassionate action through performing his duty in battle.

KARMA YOGA
(Excerpts)

Arjun said:
If it is held by you, O Janardana, that knowledge is superior to action, why then do you, O Kesava, enjoin on me this terrible action?
CH 3.1

The Blessed Lord said:
The twofold path was given by me, O sinless one, to the world in the beginning - the path of knowledge to the discerning, the path of work to the active.
CH 3.4

None can ever remain really actionless even for a moment; for everyone is helplessly driven to action by the Gunas, born of Prakriti.
CH 3.5

That deluded man is called a hypocrite who sits controlling the organs of action, but dwelling in his mind on the objects of the senses.
CH 3.6

But he excels, O Arjun, who, restraining the senses by the mind, unattached directs his organs of action to the path of work.
CH 3.7

Engage yourself in obligatory work; for action is superior to inaction, and if inactive, even the mere maintenance of your body would not be possible.
CH 3.8

Therefore, constantly perform your obligatory duty without attachment; for, by doing duty without attachment man verily obtains the Supreme.
CH 3.19

There is nought in the three worlds, O Partha, that has not been done by me, nor anything unattained that might be attained; still I engage in action.
CH 3.22

If ever I did not engage in work relentless, O Partha, men would in every respect follow my path.
CH 3. 23

These worlds would perish if I did not do action; I should be the cause of confusion of species and I should destroy these beings.
CH 3.24

As the unenlightened act from attachment to action, O Bharata, so should the enlightened act without attachment, desirous of guiding the multitude.
CH 3.25

Let not the wise man unsettle the mind of ignorant people attached to karma. By doing persistently and precisely let the wise be an example.
CH 3.26

Those deluded by the Gunas of Prakriti get attached to the functions of the Gunas. The man of perfect knowledge should not unsettle the mediocre whose knowledge is imperfect.
CH 3.29

One's own duty though imperfectly performed is better than doing another's well. Better death in doing one's duty; another's is fraught with the fear of the unknown.
CH 3.35

It is desire and wrath arising from the Rajo-Guna; all consuming, all sinful, know this as the foe here in this world.
CH 3.37

The senses, the mind and the intellect are said to be its seat; by these it deludes the embodied one, by enveloping its wisdom.
CH 3.40

Therefore, O most eminent of the Bharata race, mastering first the senses, subdue the sinful destroyer of wisdom and soul-awareness.
CH3.42

CHAPTER

4

DIVINE INCARNATION - AVATAR

'Avatar', the secret of divine incarnation revealed - Overcoming His imperishable nature to be born as a man - When morality decays He incarnates to re-establish righteousness - The Avatar remains detached therefore his actions do not bind him - In whatever way a man conceives God, He appears to him accordingly - Worshipping an Avatar is easier than realizing the Self within - The Avatar is an example for righteous behaviour - Krishna is a perfect Avatar - Krishna as an infant - Krishna as a statesman - The allegory of Krishna and Arjun - Avatar an extraordinary phenomenon.

We saw that the first chapter posed the question of how to deal with a challenging situation in life when everything appears to be at stake, through Arjun's despondency, doubt and confusion. The second introduced the concept of the eternal soul. The third explained the dynamics of action on the temporal and metaphysical planes. Now the fourth reveals an ancient secret, that of divine incarnation, which is the corrective action the Godhead takes to redeem and repair the inevitable corruption and atrophy that begins to afflict His creation.

The phenomenon of the descent of the Godhead through incarnation into the temporal world is explained with the emphasis that this has been revealed many times over the ages, first to the sun-god (the premier planetary body) onwards to Manu (the primordial man) and Ikshvaku (the first king of the solar race, (Rama's ancestor) and then to a succession of sages. However with the passage of time the knowledge decayed. Now Krishna as a favour to a special devotee whom he also deems a friend, promises to impart this precious knowledge to him. What is unique and remarkable about the Gita and Hindu beliefs in general is the relationship between the Godhead and man. God is pictured not as an old, wise, humourless, stern judge sitting on his throne in Heaven but as totally human in his incarnation on earth, youthful, warm, companionable and friendly, despite being all powerful.

This friendship emboldens Arjun to challenge Krishna's assertion that he informed Vivasvat (the sun) of this phenomenon. With his typical skepticism Arjun asks how that could be possible. Whereas the sun appeared at the beginning of creation Krishna a contemporary, was only born recently. The answer defines the distinction between an Avatar and an ordinary mortal. Krishna explains that the Avatar knows all his previous births whereas a man has no memory of them. On the issue of remembering past lives what can facilitate this is an exercise in introspection through Yoga. This helps the practitioner first to concentrate his memory on the recent past. Going deeper through practice he reaches the point of birth. There however an impenetrable barrier confronts him. But with the help of a Guru it may be possible for him to go beyond it. This is what latter day psychiatrists have sought to do with amazing recorded results.

Krishna then explains the startling facts about the manner in which the Avatar comes to be. The Godhead overcomes his nature to be eternal and imperishable and through the exercise of his magical power of illusion (Maya Shakti) is born in the temporal world as a human. We hear then the famous divine declaration in verses 7 & 8:

"Whenever there is decay of virtue and rise of lawlessness, then I embody myself, for the protection of the good and destruction of the wicked and for the establishment of Dharma. I am born from age to age."

Thus Krishna acknowledges his Avatarhood and supreme divinity but clarifies that his nature is such that he does not have any hankering for results and therefore his actions do not have the effect of binding him. His creation is after all the product of Maya, a magical and somewhat illusory world of extremes to whose machinations he is obviously impervious. He then goes further into the nature of action and inaction, a recurring theme of the Gita. Once a man abandons desire for fruits of action, then acting selflessly in a state of self control and contentment, without dependence on anything, even while acting with his body he does not 'do' anything and therefore incurs no sin. Such a man must remain content with what comes to him unsought and be balanced in success and failure. 'Acting' in this manner, he is not bound by his Karma even as the Godhead in action remains unbound and 'action less'. His Karma then dissolves and he is free from Karmic effects.

Another major theme of the Gita also emerges in this chapter, though developed more fully later: a thought on the universality of all beliefs (and religions). Krishna asserts that in whatever way a man approaches him, He accordingly responds and men pursue His path in all ways, in other words in many diverse ways, through diverse gods.

The descent of divinity in Avatarhood is one tenet of Hindu beliefs. The other is the presence of divinity in man; this is central to Hindu beliefs and is explained in the ensuing chapter.

The Avatar is important in the spiritual quest because he facilitates what otherwise would be difficult. In India divinity is seen as residing first, in every atom of creation and therefore has a ubiquitous presence. Second, It also resides within us as the Antaryami, the indweller. Finally, in an Avatar, it is in full focus. For a seeker after truth accessing the divinity within is perhaps the most difficult path. We cannot for example know what we are like until we look into a mirror - objectifying ourselves. Likewise it is difficult to sense the soul within but much easier to objectify by seeking divinity outside ourselves. It is easier to objectify divinity by worshipping an Avatar, a guru, a saint or even an idol. Objectifying divinity is easier as we are more habituated to viewing a tangible object before us than conceptualizing the intangible Atma within.

The Avatar is divinity incarnate, the rarest phenomenon if one is lucky to be a contemporary of the apostles or incarnations. But even if one is not in that happy position in this age, conceptualizing the Avatar is easier than going on a search within. The Avatar is an incarnation of the divine, different from your own earthly incarnation for the reason that the personality of the Avatar is perfect and totally harmonious with divinity whereas your personality hardly reflects any of the perfections of your Atma, the divinity within. As we are in ordinary course unable to access our Atma and make our personality conform to our true nature (Svabhava), the image and example set by the Avatar help us have a glimpse of what divinity would be like on the material plane. Thus the actions of the Avatar stand before us as the supreme example of righteous living and behaviour.

According to the scriptures, as an Avatar, Krishna possessed all sixteen attributes of perfection, that is, more perfections than other Avatars before or after. As an Avatar we find that Krishna is charming, honourable and exemplary in his behaviour at all stages of his Avatarhood. As an infant he is the epitome of adorable and charming childhood, playful and mischievous yet always displaying his supernatural divinity. For instance when his mother reprimands him for eating mud and forces his mouth open she is aghast to view the whole universe there. His pranks as an infant with other cowboys, raiding pots of butter and curd are lovable legend. Then as an adolescent his dalliance with a bevy of village damsels and cowgirls (Gopis) show the Avatar's romantic escapades, filling religious literature and music with celestial love.

Later as a prince in the epic Mahabharat he favours the forces of good represented by the Pandava brothers against their wicked and evil cousins in the great war of righteousness at Kurukshetra. He is the astute diplomat and strategist whom both sides seek alliance with. His friend Arjun, the Pandava, and the evil Kaurav prince Duryodhana vie for his support. As he lies sleeping they enter his bed chamber, Arjun humbly seating himself at Krishna's feet, Duryodhana arrogantly occupying the place next to his head, waiting for him to arise. Upon waking up his eyes naturally fall upon Arjun at his feet and he asks him to have the first choice. Duryodhan protests that he came in first and is seated next to his head therefore his must be the first rightful choice. But Krishna dismisses this claim. The choice he offers Arjun is either his individual support on condition that he will not fight in the battle or wield any weapon or the support of his mighty army and weapons. Arjun wisely chooses the lone Krishna forsaking his army. Duryodhan heaves a sigh of relief that despite first choice Arjun has foolishly forsaken what Duryodhan deems the preferred option. Arjun knows that with the Avatar beside him he needs no other support. Duryodhan skeptical of Krishna's Avtarhood is happy with the option of gaining the support of a powerful army.

Krishna in the battle becomes Arjun's charioteer. Allegorically the Avatar represents Arjun's soul and the chariot is his body. The Gita's message propounded on the battlefield of life is the message of wisdom and enlightenment emanating from his Atma.

The Avatar then is an extraordinary phenomenon. On the one hand it has the charm and charisma of a leading film star, breathtaking to view and irresistible to the surging mob of fans. On the other, he has also the dignity, majesty, serenity and power of a king of kings into whose audience you are ushered, overwhelmed and awestruck. He has also the compassion and humility of a saint, melting your ego like a candle in tears and the love of a mother you meet after years of yearning separation. He is also Superman with supernatural abilities he is loath to use but of which one is aware. This film star who happens to be a king, a saint and Superman, all rolled into one finally is also your best friend who arouses unbearable emotions of love and intimacy. If you can succeed in conceptualizing all these amazing attributes together in one person for a moment, then you can picture an Avatar standing before you. That is the image that the Hindu mind cherishes, loves and brings to life in song, verse and narrative, whether of Rama, Krishna or Buddha. The Ramayana, the Srimad Bhagawat, the Mahabharat and the Buddhist Jatakas and Sutras are replete with the doings of the Avatars, their life and message which eternally inspire and enthuse their devotees and worshipers.

GYAN KARMA SANYAS YOGA
(Excerpts)

Arjun said:
Later was your birth, earlier the birth of Vivasvat[20]; how then am I to understand that you declared it in the beginning?
CH 4.4

The Blessed Lord said:
Many are the births taken by me and you, O Arjun. I know them all while you know not, O Parantapa[21].
CH 4.5

Though I am unborn, imperishable and the Lord of beings, yet subjugating my Prakriti, I take birth by my own Maya[22].
CH 4.6

Whenever there is decay of virtue and rise of lawlessness, then I embody myself, O Bharata.
CH 4.7

For the protection of the good, for the destruction of the wicked and for the establishment of dharma[23] I am born age after age.
CH 4.8

In whatever way men seek me, in the same way do I carry out their desires; men pursue my path, O Partha, in all ways.
CH 4.11

---

20 The bright one, Surya the Sun-god.
21 Conqueror of enemies.
22 magical power of illusion.
23 Divine Order of righteous conduct and morality.

CHAPTER

5

DIVINITY WITHIN & UNITY IN DIVERSITY

Distinction between path of knowledge and path of action – There can be no renunciation without action – Knowledge and action two sides of same coin – Action does not spring from a divine source, it springs from the 'Gunas' – Selfless action builds the knowledge that facilitates the recognition of the inner Self – Then follows 'Sam Darshinah, same sightedness, recognizing that the essence is the same in all, high and low – Transcendental Monism – a supreme egalitarianism – Apparent separation of creator and creation is the product of 'Maya' and 'Ahankar', illusion engendered by ego – The realization that you are that, 'Tat Tvam Asi' – recognition of the Self within – Understanding of a difficult concept facilitated by great mystics of the 'Bhakti' movement through song and music for the common man – Yet the 'Atma' remains inconceivable.

The concept of divinity within emerges in this chapter with its corollary of unity in diversity. However the dialogue opens with a further analysis of the nature of dispassionate action. Arjun wishes to know the distinction between the path of renunciation, involving knowledge and introspection and the path of action which involves the discharge of one's duty. Once again he complains that on the one hand Krishna is telling him to renounce and on the other to act. To him this appears contradictory. Krishna explains that there is salvation in both and it is naive to separate the two for they are really one and the same. There can be no real renunciation without righteous action. The introspection and meditation in renunciation helps one realize the existence of the soul (Atma) within, stable, eternal and non-acting. On the other hand, righteous action through the body, in performance of duty, without attachment or craving fruits thereof, purifies the mind and brings peace without bondage.

It is important to realize that the dynamics of action does not emanate from the divine source, reflected in the Atma or inner Self of a being, which is eternally quiescent. It springs from its physical nature which is made up of a combination of 'Gunas', inherent traits bequeathed to the physical entity by nature (Prakriti).

Once he has this realization his mind should strive to engage in unattached action, selfless service, performance of duty, leading to self-purification and become liberated from the bondage which actions would otherwise entail (Karmic bondage). One is led to conclude that righteous action or dispassionate action (Nishkam Karma) is itself a form of renunciation.

One has to be constantly aware of the distinction between the Self, eternal and non-acting and the body, moved by its attributes and senses. The reiteration throughout the Gita that neither the Soul, which is a fragment of the divine, nor God, Prabuh are responsible for initiating man's actions or its results needs to be constantly borne in mind. Man is free and unfettered and entirely responsible for his actions and their consequences. He is free to engage in heinous crimes or the highest good uninterrupted. His life is not a deterministic puppet show, it is a path of evolution. A person who gains this realization will understand that his true Self is not acting when his senses react to sense objects.

When the senses are under control, action consists in the selfless performance of duty and knowledge begins to build leading to recognition of the true inner- Self. Then one may say that self-knowledge has dawned. This leads to the next crucial stage, that of 'same-sightedness' (Sama Darshinah), where such an enlightened man sees the same essence in the highest and the lowliest in creation: "whether that object is a Brahmin both learned and humble or an outcaste, whether a sacred cow or a dog." (Ch. 5, 18.) He then realizes that the Divine Essence (Brahman) is flawless and is the same in all and that they are all part of this Essence.

This supreme egalitarianism which defines Hindu thought, particularly Vedanta, has been called Transcendental Monism by Western scholars. Here divinity is universally dispersed in every particle of creation and this fact creates a supreme unity as well, the unity in diversity. This unity is also the Super Mind and Super Consciousness of Aurobindo[24]. It is a state realized by one personally, as much or as little, proportionate to ones striving for good through a process of adjustment and harmonious relationships with all.

Divinity is thus seen as present in man because the creator and His creation are not truly separate. The essence of the creator is present in every minute atom of his material creation. Though apparently separate, every part of creation is indivisibly conjoined in the unity of Brahman, the Universal Consciousness. The apparent separation is the result of the illusion of Maya and the emergence of 'Ahankara' or ego, the false self- consciousness, acquired by beings in the created world. The purpose of life and succeeding rebirths is to rid oneself of this false identity and realize ones intrinsic identity with the Universal Consciousness. The analogy of the spray of water drops rising high on waves in the ocean is apt. They appear separate but are part of the ocean.

There is a powerful point at the centre of all objects and beings reflecting the powerful point at the heart of creation. It is difficult to pin point where in eternity such a point could be but Hindu scriptures seek to do so symbolically. Every thing or being has a central point. In beings we call it the 'Atma' which in scientific terms is an electromagnetic centre. That centre according to the scriptures resonates with a hum, refined semantically as Om. This sound is in fact an assertion of the creative force declaring "I am". This assertion is the ultimate subjectivity. What follows automatically is the object, which is 'Sah', the 'That'. Combined it becomes "Hum-Sah", "I am that". Hindu cosmology shows

24. Great mystic Indian philosopher of the late $19^{th}/20^{th}$ century.

one of the divine trinity, Brahma, the creative force, astride a mythical swan the 'Hamsa'. Thus symbolically the creative force is asserting 'I am That'. In Pranayama, the yoga of breath control, the Guru helps the disciple in introspective concentration through inhaling with a 'Sa' and exhaling with a 'Hum', thus reminding oneself that one is That, the essential unity. Yogic practice and concentration helps the individual to fathom the centre point within him, the point which is an intrinsic part of the whole, explained in the scriptural mantra from the Brihadaraṅyaka Upanishad:

'Om Purnamadah Purnamidam Purnat Purna Mudachyate
Purnasya Purnamadaya Purnameva Vashishyate'
From that (Brahman) which is perfectly complete comes
This (phenomenal world or universe) which is perfectly complete,
From the all-perfect is produced the complete unit
Even though such a complete unit emerges from It,
Yet It remains complete and undiminished.'

Through such yogic practices one is made aware of the divinity within oneself and one's unity with creation. But to reach that level you have to strive like Mahatma Gandhi and other great personages through the ages. This is achieved as explained early in the dialogue by engaging in selfless action and the introspection and meditation of renunciation, two sides of the same coin. Then the drop rising in the air apparently separated falls back and joins the ocean.

We have seen that the concept of divinity within oneself arises from the Monist concept of a grand unity in creation right down to the minutest particle, imbued with a holy presence. Such a concept would be difficult if not impossible for an ordinary man to conceptualize. It would appear that only with years of tedious and untiring meditation even an adept Vedantin[25] schooled in Advait (non-dual) philosophy finally succeeds in conceptualizing such a grandiose portrayal of reality but it would surely be beyond

25 Practioner of Vedant philosophy – Vedant literally means 'at the end of the Vedas' and refers to teachings of the Upanishads. Shankara (AD 788-820) propounded the nondualist or Advait Vedant.

the understanding of a lay Hindu and therefore it should have no real bearing on his life and behaviour. However, quite remarkably the contrary is true. It is impressive to see that even ordinary Hindus are fully familiar with the idea of a grand unity, the ubiquitous presence of divinity and that this divinity is hidden deep within them. How did this come to pass without an established and well organized church, or philosophical training?

The Bhakti (worship with devotion and love) movement became the vehicle for passing on such difficult concepts to every home and hearth. The genius of poets and mystics of the Bhakti movement from Tulsi, Sur and Kabir to Mira, Nanak and Bulle Shah, Chaitanya, Tukaram, Vallabhcharya, Narsingh Mehta, Ravidas, Shankaracharya, Ramanuja and a host of others, carried the concepts in devotional songs (Bhajans and Geets) to the masses. The songs became no less popular than today's top ten Boliwood hit parades and to this day are widely sung and appreciated. Difficult concepts on the wings of faith and emotion became a part of popular folk music through soul stirring renditions in verse.

A song for instance spoke of a man searching for the divine, looking everywhere, in Mathura and Kashi, places of pilgrimage, in temples and shrines but found Him nowhere, till he sat quietly dejected at home and suddenly found Him glowing in his heart. Then again, the musk deer roamed the forest relentlessly in search of the heady aroma, wondering where it was coming from, little knowing that the musk was within him.

The word Antaryami, in-dweller, became synonymous with God. Kabir in his poem sang of his amusement that a fish was still thirsty though enveloped by water; man unaware of the divinity within, like the fish thirsty for water in which he is immersed. In the epic Ramayan, Hanuman is the archetypical devotee. When presented a pearl necklace by Rama's consort Sita for his unwavering loyalty and devotion, he bites into it to see if it has any value but finding no Rama in it throws it away. When asked where his Rama was, he tears open his chest to reveal him there.

However, the 'Atma' remains the most difficult concept to comprehend. It is shown as dwelling within the gross body, divine, eternal, blissful and inactive, mysterious and virtually inaccessible. The great search for divinity begins through meditation and righteous living to find it within oneself. No easy task, for it is no less than a fragment of God Himself within you but difficult to reach. When a mortal's actions approximate to the Atma's inspiration he becomes a god-man or a man of god, like Gandhi or the apostles and he is then released from the travails of material existence and re-birth. He achieves Nirvana or salvation and ultimate enlightenment.

The 'Atma' is even beyond the ethereal subtle body enveloping it. The 'Atma' is not responsible for one's physical feats – the body is responsible for that. It is not responsible for the brilliant mental processes –for that is the mind. It is not involved with extraordinary academic achievements – these arise from the intellect. It can only be sensed in great intuitive moments- moments that can produce a masterpiece like Michelangelo's 'Birth of Adam', Bach's 'Toccata and Fugue' or a 'Sermon on the Mound'. Yet it cannot be explained, described or conceptualized. Krishna himself calls it 'inconceivable'. In Chapter Two he says that some view the Soul as a marvel, others speak of it as marvelous, yet others hear of it as a wonder but though all hear of it none know it. Indeed, it remains a magnificent mystery, till one's personality approximates to it and it shines forth while still remaining unexplained.

SANYAS YOGA
(Excerpts)

Arjun said:
Renunciation of action, O Krishna, you command, and again its performance. Of the two, which is better? Tell me that conclusively.
CH 5.1

The Blessed Lord said:
Renunciation and performance of action both lead to freedom; of the two, performance of action is superior to the renunciation of action.
CH 5.2

Children not the wise speak of knowledge and performance of action as different; he who is truly established in one obtains the fruit of both.
CH 5.4

The state reached by those who renounce is also reached by men of action. He who sees that the way of renunciation and the way of action are the same, is a true seer.

CH 5.5

Renunciation is hard to attain without the yoga of action; the man of meditation, purified by the yoga of action soon attains to the enlightened state.

CH 5.6

Dedicated to the path of action with a purified mind, self disciplined and with the senses subdued one who recognizes his Self as the Self in all beings, though acting remains untainted.

CH 5.7

A yogi centred in the Self should think, 'I do nothing at all' - though seeing, hearing, touching, smelling, tasting, walking, sleeping, breathing, speaking, emptying, holding, opening and closing his eyes - firm in the thought that it is only the senses that are busy with sense objects.

CH 5.8 / 9

The yogi, abandoning attachment, performs action only with the body, the mind, the intellect and the senses, for the purification of the soul.

CH 5.11

Having mentally renounced all actions, the self-disciplined indweller rests happily in the city of nine gates, neither acting nor causing action.

CH 5.13

The Lord does not create agency or actions for the world; He does not create fruitful consequences of action; Nature does all this.

CH 5.14

Those who think of the Supreme Truth, with their Self at one with That, they get established in That, have That as their goal, cleansed of taints by knowledge, they go forth , never to return again.

CH 5.17

Men of Self-knowledge see the Eternal equally in a wise and courteous Brahman, a cow, an elephant, a dog and an outcast.

CH 5.18

They rise above this transitory existence whose minds abide in this sense of equality, for Brahman is unblemished and the same in all; such people become established in Brahman.

CH 5.19

CHAPTER

6

SANYASI - THE TRUE YOGI

The Gita is reformist - opposed to gross ritualism and asceticism into which Vedic practices degenerated - Krishna is a reformist Avatar - Tolerant and inclusive towards diverse paths of worship - Recommends Yoga as suitable for understanding unity in diversity - Humanitarianism and environmental harmony - Proper practice of Yoga - Right approach is moderation and avoiding extreme austerities - Development of same sightedness - The true Yogi is neither a recluse nor an obsessive ascetic - The Yogi who succeeds in identifying with his inner Self is a 'Sanyasi'.

The discourse in this chapter makes it quite plane that the message of the Gita was reformist, seeking to correct the gross ritualism into which the original spiritual inspiration of Vedic thought and practice had begun to degenerate. In the epic Mahabharat, Krishna appears as an Avatar who is non-conformist, whether in the romantic, strategic or ethical contexts. He is therefore particularly suited to voice the message of the reformist Gita. The Gita appears to over ride the plethora of diverse dictums and gods of the Vedas and ritualistic Hindu practices to synthesize the essence of spirit and show the true path to a confused multitude. Yet he did not preach any inalienable dogma as the only path of worship. On the contrary, later in Chapter Nine we find him referring to the many ways in which people worship Him, as one, as numerous or manifold, as gods, as ancestors, even as ghosts and demi-spirits. With supreme tolerance he asserts that by whatever method people worship, right or wrong, in fact they worship Him (Me) alone. Thus all controversies of worship are settled by the reformist Krishna through a tolerant and inclusive approach.

Here in Chapter Six the focus is on rising above ritualism through Yogic practice. Yoga is recommended as a process of gaining equanimity through harmonious thought and meditation, overcoming the restless mind and senses and reaching a state in which the aspirant begins to see himself in all beings, that is, he realizes that he is an intimate part of a complex matrix rather than a singular entity. Likewise he realizes that all beings are integral to himself i.e. he sees the essence in all and all joined together in the essence, the Godhead:

"He who sees Me everywhere and sees all in Me, he never becomes lost to Me, nor do I become lost to him". (Ch. 6, 30)

"He, who established in oneness, worships Me abiding in all beings, that yogi lives in Me, whatever may be his mode of living." (Ch.6,31)

Such a mind-set creates the right attitude for engaging in the welfare of all, a humanitarianism which is concerned about the well being not merely of mankind but the animal world as well and beyond to inanimate objects comprising nature itself, equally imbued with divinity, an attitude that would approximate to the environmental consciousness of today.

Krishna explains how such yogic practices are to be undertaken. One has to begin in solitude and with exercises to control the mind and senses. Overcoming desire, being celibate and discarding possessions, one engages in meditation, casting aside all thought, fearless and serene with the mind concentrating on the Godhead. Thus one must try and gauge the Self within, the Atma, and having felt it, rejoice in it. He repeatedly emphasizes that for achieving this, the right approach has to be one of moderation - no ascetic extremes or ritualistic excesses. Such a yogi he says must be moderate in the food he consumes, in recreation and balanced in his actions. It is quite clear that Krishna does not have an ascetic model in mind for he even allows recreation. He underlines that such a yogi is superior to ritualists, intellectuals and ascetics. He must also apply the same standards to himself as he would to others. One is reminded of the aphorism of doing unto others as you would have them do unto you. He must develop same- sightedness towards a clod of earth or a piece of gold, a friend or a foe, a sinner or a saint, with equanimity, serenity and a balanced approach.

When Arjun expresses the fear that this appears well nigh impossible, the mind being as mercurial as it is, he is reassured that through the practice of mind control and yogic meditation and constant effort it is difficult but possible. Then Arjun wishes to know if one has faith but lacks the will power to succeed, what would be the fate of such a failed practitioner. Again he is reassured that such an aspirant would achieve heavenly bliss in the hereafter and be born again in a suitably good environment to continue his efforts and shall not stand condemned. Rather such an aspirant is superior to those who engage in empty Vedic ritualism:

'...Even he who merely wishes to know of yoga rises superior to the performer of Vedic rites.' (Ch.6, 44)

In a nutshell, the yogi Krishna is speaking about is a serene, balanced individual who believes in the unity of creation, has an egalitarian approach, a focused mind, holistic understanding of the rights of all, and is humanitarian and environmentally conscious. The Yagya or sacrifice he performs is his duty, pure unqualified duty for its own sake, forsaking 'Sankalp', the desire to reap the rewards of success. Such a yogi he calls a 'Sanyasi', not the ascetic who indulges in excessive abstinence and isolates himself from the world and its cares to impose a rigorous and punishing regime on himself.

It is evident that a 'Sanyasi' in the Gita never means a recluse. 'Sankya'[26] also in the Gita has different connotations from that in the 'Sankya - Karika'[27]. Here it implies control and complete homogeneity with the elements, leading a life of righteous action, not the ascetic isolation of Sankya. Such a person performs his duty in an honest manner without obsessing about results. For facing the challenge confronting him, his mind should be stabilized, which alone will make for a sound judgment regarding the action to be taken. Krishna describes such a person as 'Yoga -

26 One of the earliest of six schools of classical Indian philosophy similar to Jainism, later assimilated in Vedic thought and the Gita.

27 Major text of Sankya philosophy.

Sudhah'[28]. His inner Self the Atma is firmly conjoined with him to give him the required force. Such a state is certainly not the result of painful penances as practiced by some ascetics. Lying on sharp iron spokes, devouring fire, or passing needles through ones tongue and other extraordinary feats which after all can also be duplicated in circuses. While one has to admit that such feats are made possible through complete bodily control and yogic breathing exercises can also help in surpassing human endurance tests, yet such feats are not the goal of the Gita. The Gita supports the satisfaction of the organs with discretion and moderation. It does not recommend such penances and clearly states that they do not help in accessing the inner Self.

The Gita also gave a different connotation to the meaning of Yoga from the traditional 'Patanjali Yoga Darshan'[29]. In modern times practitioners confuse 'Asans'(Yogic postures) and 'Pranayama' (breath control) as being synonymous with the word Yoga. In the Gita the essence of Yoga is contained in the phrase 'Yogah Karmasu Kaushalam'[30]. The word Yoga in the Gita is absolutely related to action, guided by the inner- Self or the 'still smaller voice 'of Wordsworth in his poetry or the intuitive inspiration that guides high minded activity in certain individuals.

The inner Self rests in a kind of eternity within. Once the Yogi succeeds in identifying with it, his actions assume eternal or permanent proportions, like the actions of Krishna, Buddha, Christ or Mohammad. Their actions become everlasting beacons of guidance for man acquiring an eternal quality. If one becomes firmly aligned with one's inner- Self, taking all guidance and inspiration from it, one becomes established in the eternal of which one is a part and one's Karma becomes established in eternity as those of the apostles, Avatars and Messengers. A Saṇyasi or true Yogi is one who has thus succeeded in identifying with his Atma, the inner - Self.

---

28 Adept at Yoga.

29 Sage Patanjali's compilations of yogic aphorisms - 200BC / 200AD

30 " excellence in action is Yoga".

DHYAN YOGA
(Excerpts)

The Blessed Lord said:
When one has renounced all desire for fruits of action and no longer clings to objects of the senses, then alone one is said to have attained to Yoga.
CH 6.4

A Yogi should always try to concentrate his mind living in solitude, having subdued his mind and body and got rid of desires and possessions.
CH 6.10

Serene and fearless, firm in the vow of chastity, subdued in mind, he should sit in yoga thinking on Me and intent on Me alone.
CH 6.14

Yoga is not possible for him who eats too much or for him who abstains too much from eating; it is not for him, O Arjun, who sleeps too much or too little.
CH 6.16

For him who is moderate in eating and recreation, temperate in his actions, who is regulated in sleep and wakefulness, Yoga becomes the destroyer of pain.
CH 6.17

Abandoning utterly all desires born of the selfish will and curbing by the mind all senses from all sides;

With his intellect set in firmness let him attain quietude little by little; with the mind fixed on the Self let him not think of anything.
CH 6.24 / 25

His mind being harmonized by Yoga, he sees himself in all beings and all beings in himself; he sees the same in all.
CH 6.29

He who sees Me everywhere and sees all in Me, he never becomes lost to Me, nor do I become lost to him.
CH 6.30

He who, established in oneness, worships Me abiding in all beings, that Yogi lives in Me, wheresoever he may abide.
CH 6.31

That Yogi, O Arjun, is regarded as the supreme, who judges pleasure and pain everywhere by the same standard as he applies to himself.
CH 6.32

Arjun said:
This Yoga of equanimity, taught by you, O Madhusudan - I do not see any stability for it, because of restlessness of the mind.
CH 6.33

The Blessed Lord said:
Doubtless, O mighty-armed, the mind is restless and hard to control; but by practice and non-attachment, O son of Kunti, it can be controlled.
CH 6.35

Arjun said:
What of the man possessed of faith but lacking self-control, whose mind deviates from Yoga, what end does he meet with, O Krishna, having failed to attain perfection in Yoga?
CH 6.37

The Blessed Lord said:
O Partha, Neither in this world nor in the next is there destruction for him; for, the doer of good, O my son, Never comes to grief.
CH 6.40

Having attained to the worlds of the righteous and having lived there countless years, he who falls from Yoga is reborn in the house of the pure and prosperous.
CH 6.41

There he regains the knowledge acquired in his former body and he strives more than before for perfection, O joy of Kurus[31].
CH 6.43

By that very former practice he is led on in spite of himself. Even he who merely wishes to know of Yoga rises superior to the performer of mere rituals of worship.
CH 6.44

The Yogi is deemed superior to ascetics, superior to men of knowledge even; he is also superior to ritualists. Therefore be you a Yogi, O Arjun.
CH 6.46

31 The Kuru clan comprised the warring Kauravas and Pandavas - Krishna regarded Arjun as the finest of the Kurus. The great Mahabharat battle took place on the field of Kurukshetra in present day Haryana State.

CHAPTER

7

GOD AND NATURE

There are two aspects of God's nature - The lower is the material world, the higher is the ubiquitous spiritual essence - The universal essence also manifests as procreative desire - Those engaged in evil are not interested in truth - Types of spiritually inclined people with diverse motives - He strengthens faith of all worshippers, however limited their understanding.

Krishna now wishes Arjun to know him in full, in his manifold totality. This includes two aspects of his nature, the lower and the higher. The lower is in fact the material world and includes earth, water, fire, air ether (i.e. the elements), mind, intellect and ego, called Prakriti. The higher nature is the all pervading life principle, the ubiquitous spiritual essence, Brahman. Both aspects are integrated in His creation and in man, the one, as the body, the other, as the soul, the one is nature as unconscious matter, the other, the conscious spirit infusing it. The inner-Self is a part and a reflection of the Over-Self, the original seed of all which is described as Adi-Chaitanya, the original consciousness, the great kinetic force of the universe.

When that original essence asserted itself with a self-conscious 'I am', as mentioned earlier, its supreme subjectivity automatically produced objectivity, the 'Big Bang' of creation. This universal kinetic force also manifests itself as 'Kama', procreative desire. Krishna accepts that He is the desire in beings, not contrary to righteous behaviour (Dharma) : "...dharmaviruddho bhuteshu kamo 'smi..." (Chp. 7, 11). At a lower level that desire is sex, the moving force of all elements. Sex is not opposed to nature or religion.

However relying on this verse, several cults cropped up enjoining free sex in the name of Krishna worship. This is my view is not sanctioned. Krishna has stated earlier that all consuming desire is sinful and veils the wisdom of the Atma.

Krishna, after providing a philosophical and metaphysical insight into reality, then proceeds to illustrate the universal presence in all things in some of the most poetical and startlingly beautiful verses in the Gita. He is the flavour of water, the radiance in the Sun and Moon, the resonance of sound, virility in man, fragrance in earth, brilliance in fire, intelligence of the intelligent, splendour of the splendid, strength of the strong, desire in beings, the combination of attributes (Gunas) that distinguish beings.

He then explains the type of people who seek him and those who do not. Those engaged in evil, deluded and lacking in discrimination, overwhelmed by the illusory world are not interested in seeking the truth and do not seek him.

Those who do, he cautions are of many types and with different spiritual priorities. There are the desperate beings, badly hit by misfortune, who wish to be alleviated from their suffering. Others are academic seekers after knowledge, disputing Being, Non-Being and a greater cohesive Being. Others perform 'Pujas', ritual prayers to propitiate the gods for wealth and material benefits and lastly there are the wise who try to know Him through intuitive intellect and meditation. While the last are the best, all engaged in any type of spiritual activity, remain a good example for the multitude. He therefore strengthens the faith of all worshippers, however limited their purpose.

This reiterates the dictum pronounced in Chapter 3: "Na buddhibhadam janayed agyanam karma sanginam" (Ch. 3, 26) - let not the wise man create confusion (by high flown lectures) in the minds of ignorant people attached to karma. They should be left alone with their limited spirituality, content in worshipping their gods. They obtain their limited goals, worshipping a limited form of His, which are of course facilitated by Him alone. However, He admits that few know His true nature. Most regard him, Krishna, as a mere human. They do not recognize the Avatar nor do they see that he is a manifestation of the unmanifest essence of Godhead.

GYAN VIGYAN YOGA
(Excerpts)

The Blessed Lord said:
My nature is divided eightfold - Earth, water, fire, ether, mind, intellect and ego.
CH 7.4

This is My lower nature, but different from it, know, O mighty armed, My higher nature - the soul element by which this universe is upheld.
CH 7.5

Know that from these two are sprung all beings. I am also the origin and the dissolution of the whole universe.
CH 7.6

I am the taste in water, O son of Kunti, I am the radiance in the moon and the sun; I am the syllable Om in the Vedas; sound in ether and manhood in man.
CH 7.8

I am the sweet fragrance in the earth and the brilliance in fire; I am the life in all born beings and the austerity of the ascetics.
CH 7.9

Know me , O Partha, as the eternal seed of all beings; I Am the intelligence of the intelligent; the splendour of the splendid.
CH 7.10

I am the might of the mighty, devoid of desire and passion. In beings, I am desire, not contrary to Dharma, O chief of the Bharatas.
CH 7.11

This divine illusion of Mine, made up of the Gunas, is hard to surmount; but those who take refuge in Me alone; they cross over this illusion.
CH 7.14

Those engaged in evil, the deluded, the basest of men, deprived of discrimination by Maya and pursuing demonic ways, do not seek refuge in Me
CH 7.15

Four kinds of virtuous men worship me, O Arjun; the distressed, the seekers after knowledge, the seekers after wealth and the wise, O best of the Bharatas.
CH 7.16

Noble indeed are all these; but the wise man, I deem, to be My very Self. For, steadfast in mind, he is established in Me alone, as the supreme goal.
CH 7.18

At the end of many births, the man of wisdom takes refuge in Me, realizing that Vasudeva is all that is. Rare indeed is that great soul.
CH 7.19

But those whose discrimination has been led astray by this or that desire seek refuge in other gods, following this or that rite, constrained by their own nature.
CH 7.20

Whatever divine form any devotee with faith wishes to worship, that same faith in him I make unwavering.
CH 7.21

Endowed with that faith, he engages in the worship of that form and from it obtains his desires, which are actually being ordained by Me.
CH 7.22

But the fruit that accrues to those men of small intellect is finite. The worshippers of the gods go to the gods; My devotees come to Me.
CH 7.23

CHAPTER

8

COSMOLOGY OF THE SPIRIT

Essential themes of Hindu cosmology - Adhibhuta: physical and elemental aspect of God - Adhyatma: Self- knowledge through meditation - Adhidaiva: ubiquitous essence of God - Adhiyagya: life long striving for Self knowledge and ethical perfection - Brahma's unmanifest creative soup is also finite - Beyond that is the imperishable unmanifest plane, His 'Supreme abode' - Imperfect efforts at self-realization will result in rebirth.

In this chapter further details are provided of the essential themes of Hindu Cosmology and metaphysics. In the previous chapter Arjun had a glimpse of God's nature consisting of the perishable physical aspect of creation and the imperishable universal essence present in the body as the soul. The new terms used in this chapter need further elucidation. Arjun wishes to know what is meant by Adhibhuta, Adhyatma, Adhidaiva, Adhiyagya and Karma.

The first Adhibhuta is the physical and elemental aspect of God referred to in the previous chapter. It is perishable and therefore not a perfect inspiration for action and thought as it is conditioned not by spirit but by the qualities of genes and chromosomes inherited by one from parentage. It reflects the physical force of the genetic field. But it is not one's own true intrinsic nature, the 'Svabhava'. That true nature is the Great Spirit within that inspires the best in us, a beacon pointing to what is good, lasting and beautiful. But its call is often superseded by external forces such as the genetic pressures of heredity, pride and prejudice arising from ego and intellectual activity which is not connected with the spirit. It is through 'Sadhana', perseverance, right living and meditation that we come to realize our 'Svabhava' and this self - knowledge is Adhyatma. It is further explained that the imperishable eternal spiritual essence, here termed Brahman (not the Brahma of the trinity) has an innate impulse to inhabit physical nature and it is thereby ubiquitous. The process of inhabiting the individual body as the soul is also called Adhyatma.

Adhidaiva is the cosmic soul or consciousness, also called Purush which inhabits the physical and spiritual universe, the ubiquitous essence of Godhead. Adhiyagya is the enabling sacrifice in the body, continuing throughout life, the tireless striving for ethical perfection and self-knowledge, which at death facilitates merger with the Super-Soul (Paramatma), thus finally, helping that individual's soul to gain cosmic consciousness. Adhiyagya is His supreme undiluted essence and is the finest core of one's being, finer than life itself. Thus Krishna at the very beginning of the discourse asserts that He is Adhiyagya. The act of creation is Karma with a big K in the sense of it being the original act from which all acts stem and flow.

Arjun is then told that the apparently limitless creation is itself finite and even Brahma's[32] days and nights which encompass more than a thousand ages are numbered and ultimately terminate when all created beings merge into an unmanifest state from which they re-emerge when the next cycle commences. But beyond that unmanifest creative soup from which beings and creation emerge time and again and dissolve back into, is another unmanifest reality which is truly eternal and imperishable, not effected by the cyclic movement of the Brahma universes. This 'beyond beyond state' of the unmanifest imperishable is the ultimate goal (not Brahma's unmanifest plane) and once a being attains to this plane, he does not return. That plane or state is His supreme abode (Param Dham).

Having worked throughout life to discover his true nature, 'Svabhava' and successfully accessing the essence within, at the

32 God of the Hindu triad: the creative power Brahma, distinct from Brahman the Universal Divine Essence.

end of life such an adept enters the effulgence of His supreme spirit. However, if the seeker's efforts are not perfect and lack in resolve with concentration wavering, the great effulgence of the supreme spirit will also be diminished and bedimmed. Such a person will be guided to a desirable re-birth, to enable him to continue the quest. Here one is reminded of the following verse:

"The bright and the dark, these paths are deemed to be the worlds eternal paths; by the one a man goes not to return, by the other he returns again"(Ch.8, 25)

AKSHAR BRAHMA YOGA
(Excerpts)

Arjun said:
What is Brahman? what is Adhyatma? What is Karma? O best among men! what is said to be Adhibhuta and what is called Adhidaiva?
CH 8.1

Who dwells in our body as the agent of sacrifice. O Madhusudan? and how, at the time of death art thou to be known by the self-controlled?
CH 8.2

The blessed Lord said:
The imperishable is Brahman, the supreme. His dwelling in the individual body is called Adhyatma. The offering which causes the origin of beings is called Karma.
CH 8.3

Adhibhuta is perishable nature and the cosmic spirit is the Adhidaivatva; I alone am Adhiyagya, the sacrifice in this body, o best of the embodied.
CH 8.4

All the worlds including that of Brahma are subject to return, O Arjun; but on reaching me, O son of Kunti, there is no rebirth.
CH 8.16

Those who know that the days of Brahma lasts a thousand Ages and that his night lasts a thousand ages, they are the knowers of day and night.
CH 8.17

At the coming of day all manifest beings proceed from the unmanifest and at the coming of night they merge again in the same which is called the unmanifest.
CH 8.18

But beyond this unmanifest, there is yet another unmanifest eternal existence which does not perish even when all existence perish.
CH 8.20

This unmanifest is called the imperishable; It is said to be the ultimate goal. Those who attain to it return not. This is my supreme Abode.
CH 8.21

CHAPTER

9

A REMARKABLE TOLERANCE TOWARDS DIVERSE PATHS OF WORSHIP

His essence is everywhere, in all things and beings - But every unit of creation does not contain His totality - He animates His nature time and again to create the world and dissolve it from age to age - This is done with detachment; supreme example of undifferentiated action - All beings are the same for Him, none dear none hateful - He acknowledges that different types of belief systems exist - He does not condemn or deny them in favour of one dogma - Avers that all lead to Him through diverse paths - Gita's supreme tolerance in an age of bigotry - Even repentant sinners can achieve enlightenment - Enlightenment is possible for all irrespective of caste or gender.

In the previous chapters Krishna has dealt with numerous issues both material and spiritual; the body and its inhabiting soul, the significance of action, the relationship between the individual and the cosmos, the soul and the super-soul, rebirth and reincarnation as Avatar, the ubiquitous presence of the spiritual essence and the need for a Yogi to access his innermost being and with its support establish communion with the cosmic consciousness gaining a permanent state of enlightenment, free from the travails of re-birth.

In this chapter He reiterates that His unmanifest Self is everywhere and sustains everything and likewise everything is part of His universal essence, yet when looking at the individual unit of creation, His totality is not contained within it, just as a drop of water thrown out of the ocean is a part of it but it is not the ocean.

He animates His nature, Prakriti, time and again to create numerous beings and objects which remain governed by His natural laws. At the end of an age, creation dissolves back into His nature. Thus through the cyclical bursts of creative activity, the physical world is created and dissolved time and again.

He is quick to point out that this spontaneous recurrent creative activity does not create any attachment in Him and He remains calm and unmoved, not bound by His acts. He is after all the initiator of the first Karma and the supreme role model for unattached, dispassionate action.

He adopts a supremely egalitarian approach towards all beings, asserting that for Him all beings are the same, none dear and none hateful. The creator is even handed, balanced and tolerant, qualities that make him merciful.

It is therefore not surprising that the Gita, time and again, displays a unique tolerance towards all forms of worship. Krishna describes to Arjun all manner of persons inhabiting his creation from skeptics whose descent to the darkness is certain, to great wise souls, the perfect Yogis, those who worship one undivided consciousness (non-Dualism), to those who separate god, the soul and the world into distinct entities (Dualism), to devotees who worship gods and yet others who worship ancestors and ghosts (Ch.9.15). He is not disparaging of these worshipers even as earlier He had cautioned wise men from desisting from confusing simple minded people with wisdom beyond their understanding. In fact He avers that all these diverse worshippers, in their different ways worship Him alone, though by unorthodox means and deviant routes. Earlier it will be recalled He had stated that He strengthens the faith of people whatever way they identify with Him in prayer, and fulfills their spiritual aspirations (Ch.7.20 to 22).

It is quite remarkable that in an age of bigotry and narrowly defined religious dogma who breach could invite excommunication, ostracism and even stern punishment, the Gita should be not merely acknowledging diversity of faith and practice but sanctioning it as acceptable paths to the same goal with the only reservation that limited or inferior practices would produce limited results: "

worshippers of the Devas (demi-gods) go to the Devas (their realms), worshipers of the ancestors go to the ancestors, and spirit worshippers go to the ghosts and spirits they worship, My worshippers come to me". Of all the worshippers, Yogis, ritualists, academics, the best are the Yogis who meditate on Him.

The tenor of tolerance, even handedness and detachment are qualities of the Supreme Spirit which emerge clearly and impressively. While creating the world He is calm and detached. In dealing with the constituents of His creation He underlines that there are no original favourites or despicable Satans. The one who meditates upon Him as a Yogi finds supreme acclaim in that he quickly merges with Him, so to speak, in a divine embrace. Likewise He tolerates diversity in beliefs, emphasizing that even by other methods of worship, people can attain His grace. There is to be no condemnation and denial of practices and beliefs in favour of one dogma or practice. What exquisite tolerance when one looks around and finds that religious intolerance has been the scourge of history past and very much in the present as well.

In the same liberal vein the discourse concludes with the reminder that even a great sinner who repents and adopts a righteous path will soon achieve lasting peace and become a great soul, for "my devotees never perish". Even in those ancient times when gender equality was unknown and the caste system was sanctioned by orthodox tradition, the Gita had the courage to assert that people belonging to inferior castes or women even, would attain the supreme goal if they sought His refuge in worship. Touchingly He promises his devotees that whatever he offers him, be it a leaf, a flower, a fruit or just water, with love and devotion, that he surely accepts.

Like in chapter seven once again we are treated to poetic illustrations of the nature of God. The complex philosophical concepts are simplified for the understanding of all: He is the father, the mother, the grandsire of the world. He is the goal, the supporter, the Great Lord, the witness, the abode, the shelter, the friend, the origin, the dissolution, the foundation and the seed imperishable. This beautiful explanation meets every man's image of the creator.

Philosophers of Existentialism, like Albert Camus and Jean Paul Sartre have explained elaborately the Nihilism afflicting the modern mind. Albert Camus has dramatized a person in utter fear of being killed who becomes desperate and cynical about his very existence before the final hour. Sartre goes on in the same strain, illustrating the pains and pleasures of existence till the moment of non-being arrives leaving him in the great and gory darkness of the Nihilist. The Yogi too doubtless shall walk into darkness at death but with a beacon of light of the Super-Being. As the Shastric aphorism asserts:

'Asato ma sat gamaya, Tamaso ma jyotir gamaya, Mrityor ma amritam gamaya'

From untruth you will attain truth, from darkness you will proceed to light, from death you will attain immortality.

RAJAVIDYA RAJGUHYA YOGA
(Excerpts)

The Blessed Lord said:

All this universe is pervaded by Me in My unmanifested form; All beings exist in Me but I do not abide in them.
CH 9.4

And yet the beings do not dwell in Me. Behold My divine mystery, My spirit which is the source of all beings, sustains the beings but does not abide in them.
CH 9.5

When an age-cycle ends, O son of Kunti, all beings enter into my Nature; when the next age-cycle begins I generate them again.
CH 9.7

Animating my Nature, I send forth again and again all this helpless mass of beings under the power of Nature.
CH 9.8

But these acts bind me not, O winner of wealth, for I remain unconcerned and unattached to these acts.
CH 9.9

Under My supervision, Nature produces all this, the moving and the unmoving, and thus the world revolves, O son of Kunti.
CH 9.10

Yet others sacrifice with the Yagya of knowledge and worship Me in various ways as the one, as several or as diverse with many facets.
Ch 9.15

I am the father of this world, the mother, the sustainer and the grandsire; I am the object of knowledge, the purifier, the syllable Om and the three Vedas[33].
CH 9.17

I am the goal, the supporter, the Lord, the Witness, the abode, the shelter, the friend, the Origin, the dissolution, the foundation, the treasure house and the seed imperishable.
CH 9.18

Even those devotees who, with faith, worship other gods, worship Me alone, O son of Kunti, by a contrary method.
CH 9.23

Worshippers of the gods go to the gods; worshippers of the ancestors go to the ancestors; worshippers of the ghosts go to the ghosts; but those who worship Me come to Me.
CH 9.25

Whoever offers Me with devotion, a leaf, a flower, a fruit or water, I accept that pious offering of the heart.
CH 9.26

I am the same to all beings; to Me there is none hateful, none dear. But those who worship Me with devotion, they are in Me and I also am in them.
CH 9.29

Even if a man of the most sinful conduct worships Me with undeviating devotion, he must be reckoned as righteous, for he has rightly resolved.
CH 9.30

Soon he becomes a man of righteousness and obtains lasting peace. O son of Kunti, know for certain that My devotee never comes to harm.
CH 9.31

For those who take refuge in Me, O Partha, though they be of inferior birth - women, merchants, farmers and slaves - even they attain the Supreme Goal.
Ch 9.32

33 Ancient Hindu scriptures: Rig, Sam and Yajur Vedas - 1000 - 1500BC

CHAPTER

10

THE GLORIOUS ATTRIBUTES OF GOD

How is one to conceive God - What are His attributes - He is the Self, Atma, in all beings, the source and the end of all, the finest qualities in man arise from him, He is the best in all categories - No limits to his definition - But what need is there to explain Himself.

Time and again Arjun has been told that he must meditate upon the Universal Essence, now incarnated as Krishna. He must be devoted to Him, make Him his supreme goal, worship Him and thereby he will eventually merge with Him. He has learnt that his innermost essence is a fragment of God and if one is identified with it at the time of death one would see the great Supreme Consciousness filling up the darkness which threatens the dying.

Arjun wishes to know how he is to conceive God in his meditations, what are His attributes, His powers and the glory of His divinity by which He is to be identified. In a beautiful verse he says: "...tell me, for you alone know Yourself by Yourself, O first among men, O source of all beings, O lord of all beings, O God of Gods, O ruler of the world".

He acknowledges having often heard from Krishna and other wise men that He is the Supreme Consciousness, unmanifest in eternity as also the manifest reality, the universal essence in every thing manifest and unmanifest, the purity in a person, the embodiment of the divine, the primeval God, unborn and omnipresent. Arjun remembers that Krishna is often critical of those who regard him as mortal, failing to see that the Avatar is the unmanifest making itself manifest for the amelioration of mankind and His created world. Thus he now urges Krishna to tell him "again in detail" about His attributes His power and glory.

The resounding answer comes from the mouth of the Avatar complimenting what Arjun has already observed. He is the Self, Atma situated in all beings. He is the beginning, the middle and the end of all beings, in other words they emerge from Him, are sustained in life by Him and dissolve into Him at the close. Though Himself, He is unborn and without a beginning, the lord of all the worlds. He is the seed of all beings and all devouring death as well. Qualities and attributes in man arise from His essence which include intellect, wisdom, clarity of thought, compassion and forgiveness, patience, truth, self-restraint, calmness, also pain and pleasure, birth and death, fear and fearlessness, non-violence (Ahimsa), equanimity, contentment, austerity, charity and fame and infamy. Poetically he adds that the prosperity of the prosperous, fame, fortune, speech, memory, intelligence, constancy and forbearance also proceed from his grace. He then proceeds to identify the best in every category, from sages to scriptures, to gods, to mountains, to oceans, to trees to beasts and birds, to worshippers, to literature and grammar, all being representative of his glory. He adds that there is no limit to the attributes that define him and this is only a brief example of his glory.

Then as if speaking to himself, he adds a delightful footnote to the chapter; why is he telling Arjun all this. What need of this detailed explanation? After all he is the creator of the universe and what need is there to explain himself to his own constituent?

VIBHUTI YOGA
(Excerpts)

The Blessed Lord said:
He who knows Me as unborn and without origin as the Great Lord of the worlds, he among mortals is not deluded and is freed from sins.
CH 10.3

Intellect, wisdom, non -delusion, patience, truth, self restrain, calmness, pleasure, pain, birth, death, fear and fearlessness; non -violence, equanimity, contentment, austerity, charity, fame and ill-repute - these different qualities of beings arise from Me alone.
CH 10.4 / 5

I am the origin of all; from Me all things evolve. The wise know this and adore Me with all their heart.
CH 10. 8

Arjun said:
You are the Supreme Brahman, the Supreme Abode, the Supreme Purifier, the Eternal, Divine soul, the Primeval God, the Unborn, the Omnipresent.
CH 10.12

Only You alone know Yourself by yourself, O Supreme One, O Source of beings, O Lord of beings, O God of gods, O Ruler of the world.
CH 10.15

So tell me without reserve of your divine glories by which you pervade all these worlds.
CH 10.16

Tell me again in detail, O Janardana, of your yoga powers and attributes; for I am not satiated with hearing your life - infusing words.
CH 10.18

The blessed Lord said:
Very well! I shall now tell you of My divine powers according to their prominence, O best of Kurus; for there is no end to the details of My manifestations.
CH 10.19

I am the Self, O Gudakesh[34], seated in the hearts of all beings, I am the beginning, the middle and also the end of all beings.
CH 10.20

Of created things, I am the beginning and the end and also the middle, O Arjun. Of sciences the science of the Self; Of those who debate I am reason.
CH 10.32

Of letters I am the letter A, of compound words I am the dual. I am imperishable Time. I am the provider facing all ways.
CH 10.33

---

34 One who has control over his sleep - Arjun could go without sleep for days.

I am all devouring Death. I am the prosperity of the prosperous; of feminine qualities I am Fame, Fortune, Speech, Memory, Intelligence, Constancy and Forgiveness.
CH 10.34

I am the gambling of the tricksters, I am the splendour of the splendid; I am victory; I am effort; I am the goodness of the good.
CH 10.36

Of those who subdue I am the sword and the rod; Of those who seek victory I am strategy; Of secrets I am silence; and I am the wisdom of the wise.
CH 10.38

I am the seed of all beings, O Arjun; There is no being, whether moving or unmoving, that can exist without Me.
CH 10.39

There is no limit to my divine powers, O harasser of foes; only in part have I declared to you the extent of My glory.
CH 10.40

Whatsoever is glorious, graceful, or powerful; know that to have sprung from a fragment of my splendour.
CH 10.41

But what need is there, O Arjun, for this detailed knowledge? I stand supporting the whole universe with a single fragment of myself.
CH 10.42

CHAPTER

11

VISION OF THE COSMIC FORM

Arjun, not satisfied with the abundant spiritual insights revealed to him, now desires to see God's cosmic form - No similar attempt in visualizing God's universal form in any other spiritual literature - A mind blowing vision unfolds - Krishna confers 'celestial eyes' on Arjun to enable him to see and withstand the mind shattering vision of the cosmic colossus - Arjun apologizes for having treated Krishna with familiarity as a companion and friend in jest and at play - Unable to bear the magnitude of the overwhelming vision he requests that Krishna resume His earthly form - Krishna resumes His mortal form and consoles the bewildered Arjun.

Arjun is now full of knowledge. He knows that the body and its natural environment, the physical universe is all perishable. He knows that the Soul which is imperishable and eternal inhabits the body. It sallies forth at death only to re-inhabit another body, with a different personality, going from life to life virtually endlessly. He knows that the Soul is part of the Universal Essence, a cosmic consciousness that creates and recreates physical universes which dissolve back into it eventually. He knows that the goal of life is to access the Soul within through the Yoga of worship and meditation and righteous selfless performance of duty and that when this is achieved with perfection and the personality becomes fully aligned with the Soul, then the Soul finds release from rebirth and merges back into that Universal Consciousness. It is as if the Soul's task is to refine gross matter and having done that it merges back into its true essence. He knows also that the Supreme Consciousness is compassionate enough to suffer reincarnating itself as an Avatar on the physical plane, experiencing the same pleasure and pain as ordinary beings. He knows that it does this to correct the inevitable atrophy and deterioration which begin to afflict His creation. He has also been told of the amazing attributes of that divine consciousness.

Yet all this abundant information remains somewhat academic. All the metaphysical, philosophical and poetical explanations fail to satisfy the urge to experience it through being afforded a grand vision of this reality. As they rightly say, 'seeing is believing'. We cannot blame him for this childlike desire to see it. We too would do likewise in a similar situation.

In modern times a child may also find information about the planet earth, the solar system, the galaxy and nebulae to be quite academic, till he is shown a photograph of the splendid blue planet taken from Apollo on a Moon mission from space or if he were to breathlessly view the amazing universe in a planetarium, mouth ajar. The eleventh chapter is that extraordinary spiritual planetarium of yesteryear, daring to show a vision of a universal God beyond our remotest imagination. In no other religious literature that I am aware of has such a daring effort been undertaken. Michelangelo's 'Last Judgment' at the Sistine Chapel in Rome is a close if marvelous approximation, though limited to heaven and hell. Modern day Science Fiction has also been boldly imaginative seeking to give meaning to the theory of relativity in time and space in Arthur C. Clerks '2001 a Space Odyssey', where time stands still for the cosmonaut as he moves through space at the speed of light, while the earth he returns to has aged beyond recognition. Later in 'Childhood's End', Clerk's genius visualizes a universal consciousness forming out of myriad released souls.

But here, in an ancient Hindu scripture, a vision of that Universal Consciousness at play in a physical and spiritual cosmos is simply overwhelming in its scope and magnitude even before the imagination could have been stirred by the maturing of science and astronomy. Indian miniature paintings sought bravely to depict pictorially that vision of the Gita with charming naivety but it is the words of the Gita that succeed in shaking one to the soul. Not

Arjun alone but the reader also experiences a mind blowing vision as the phenomenon unfolds before them! That universal image of the Gita, germinating through the Upanishads, has become embedded in the Hindu psyche like a mysterious monolith, the 'Virat' Universal form of God, the micro and the macro of Quantum Physics rolled into one! We in India forever remain keen, like Arjun, to be enthralled and overwhelmed by the mind shattering divine vision of the glorious if fearful Universal Form.

For me this is the most vivid and enthralling spiritual spectacle, of a piece with say, witnessing the 'Sermon on the Mound', the fiery descent of the 'Ten Commandments' before Moses, then Jesus on the cross before a sky blazing with wrathful lightening as he pleads with his 'Father', 'forgive them for they know not what they do', or prince Siddhartha in meditation under the banyan tree, resisting temptations as enlightenment dawns in a halo behind his head transforming him into the Buddha (even if only in a Hollywood movie).

Arjun here is being real cute and careful in his pleadings. First, with a hint of flattery, he expresses his profound gratitude for the discourses on the origin and dissolution of beings and of his beloved Lord's 'inexhaustible greatness'. He acknowledges this lovingly, by calling Krishna 'lotus eyed' and quickly if not so credulously asserting that his delusion has now been dispelled. Then as it were, tentatively he allows, 'as you have declared so it is', but there appears to linger some dissatisfaction. Then summoning courage he blurts out: 'yet I desire to see your sovereign form'. Then he is afraid that he may have asked for too much and qualifies it by adding: 'if you O lord think it possible for me to see it, then do....show me your eternal form'.

Here we get a glimpse again of a person who suddenly discovers that his beloved boon companion is no ordinary mortal as he so charmingly admits later after observing the unique and fearful, earth shattering vision. At the close of the chapter he apologizes for having rashly and carelessly or out of friendly love failed to give him due respect: "O Krishna, O Yadav, O friend, looking upon you merely as a friend.... in whatever way I may have insulted you in jest, while at play, reposing, sitting or at meals, when alone or in company, for that I implore you to forgive me'. One can imagine the jesting at play, the back slapping, the intimate companionship at meals or in repose. To have God as your pal! For God to allow you to treat Him as a friend and for him to treat you with such intimacy - one is left speechless and charmed by the Hindu conception of God incarnate.

"But you cannot see me with these eyes of yours" replies Krishna. Here I am reminded of 'The Black Cloud', a Science Fiction novel by astrophysicist Fred Hoyle about a mysterious cloud that arrives above the Earth. Scientists struggle to decipher its message and finally receive from it the technology to communicate with it. They set up the apparatus as instructed. It wishes to communicate knowledge about itself and the mysterious universe to any representative. A volunteer is seated before the instrument panel and he is connected to it. As the information comes in, the volunteer's brain cannot handle the complexity and overload, resulting in his brain short circuiting into insanity. Likewise, limited by our mental capabilities, one can only absorb so much of reality and make sense of it. Scientists are familiar with the mysteries of Quantum Physics but can they truly comprehend it to make sense of it for us in our daily lives? Astronomers can conceptualize Black Holes and Supernovas but can they comprehend them in their totality? When a concept goes beyond our understanding we seek to symbolize it mathematically as a convenient way of simplifying the ultra-complex. A simple equation, E=MC square, makes us feel we have understood the inconceivable.

We need giant telescopes to look at distant cosmic phenomena, electronic microscopes to look at the subatomic world, computers to engage in complicated math to understand Quantum facts. No wonder Krishna realizes the severe limitations not only of human vision but of the human mind as well. He alone 'knows Himself by Himself' as Arjun puts it. But Arjun is a dear disciple and friend and his request has to be honoured. Therefore through his generosity and magical Yogic powers (Yoga Kshemum), Krishna confers divine sight on him - celestial eyes (Divyam Chakshuhu).

Then, before him, now looking through the divine protective facility of celestial eyes, Arjun sees his friend and companion the charming Avatar Krishna begin to metamorphose into a cosmic colossus with hundreds of thousands of shapes glowing with a myriad colours. He sees the whole universe and everything else there is to see integrated within the form. One of the most beautiful passages of the Gita follows:

"If the splendour of a thousand suns were to blaze forth all at once in the sky, that would be like the splendour of that mighty being. There in the body of the God of Gods he then saw the whole universe with its many divisions drawn together into one" (Ch. XI- 12/13)

Even the one sun in our world is so brilliant that were we to stare at it we would be blinded, though we like to bask in its light and warmth. The radiance of a thousand suns shining at once is beyond conception - it would be death to look upon such brilliance. Therefore Arjun was fortunate to have the filter of divine sight to sustain the experience and enjoy such mind blowing brilliance of the Super Conscious Essence.

The form adopted to show Arjun the universal vision was necessarily anthropomorphic, with eyes, mouths, heads, hands and legs, the multiple colossi stretching all ways. Doubtless to safeguard against jolting him into insanity like the one suffered by our Science fiction volunteer with the mysterious cloud. But in fact a form was not relevant to the content which conveyed the substance of the message of divine reality. Arjun remarks that he sees an infinity of forms on all sides without a beginning a middle or an end. We cannot then think in terms of one form only. He sees the 'sun and the moon in the eyes', in other words the planetary systems and the physical universe. He sees beings flowing into him in the fires of dissolution and beings flowing out in the catharsis of creation.

Arjun is overwhelmed and fearful and his hair stands on end (Romanchit). Trembling, he confesses that looking upon this awesome reality he is bewildered and fearful. Yet he is courageous enough to ask: "Who are you, I know not your purpose and desire to know you". The vision has not sated his curiosity, rather he now dares to ask that cosmic colossi 'without beginning or middle or end' and planetary systems orbiting in what must be His eyes, who He is! Like a courageous soldier he demands to know Him. For that mighty eternal colossus the impertinence of the puny but brave soul must have been endearing.

From that radiating cosmic vision comes a deep sonorous reply:

"I am the mighty world destroying time"

He doesn't say much more. In the Gita, rather than the universal form speaking of His infinite greatness, it is Arjun who overawed, begins to describe Him. Wide eyed he calls out: " You are the primal cause, abode of the universe, the imperishable, the being and the non-being, the primal god, the ancient one, the one who pervades the universe, the adorable, the greatest Guru" and implores his forgiveness for his inadvertent transgressions and presumptuous behavior as a friend, asking the Lord to be compassionate "as a father to a son, a friend to a friend and as a lover to his beloved" (not overawed enough to give up friendship and love).

He admits that while he "rejoices" at having seen what has never been seen before he is confounded with fear at what he is witnessing and can no longer bear to look upon such immense glory and fearful splendour and pleads that he would once again like to see his mortal friend. How very touching the melodramatic scene must have been.

Thereupon the Great Lord, as it were, collapses in a moment the 'Virat' form with the brightness of a thousand suns (in India this is a very common name - Virat), resuming his gentle form, first as the intermediate four armed celestial Vishnu and then further devolving into the earthly, mortal form of the Avatar, the gentle Krishna, touchingly consoling and comforting the terrified Arjun, known to him endearingly as Partha. The wonderful Arjun, quite like a Greek hero, courageous and righteous, rejoices on seeing his own familiar gentle friend Krishna once again.

VISHVARUP DARSHAN YOGA
(Excerpts)

Arjun said:
By this profound discourse concerning the self, which you have delivered out of compassion for me, my delusion has been dispelled.
CH 11.1

Even as You have declared yourself , so it is. But i wish to look upon your sovereign form, O Lord supreme.
CH 11.3

If you. O Lord, think it possible for me to see it, then do, O Lord of yoga, show me your Eternal form.
CH 11.4

The Blessed Lord said:
Behold , O Partha, the hundreds and the thousands of My forms, diverse, divine various of colour and shape.
CH 11.5

Behold now, O Gudakesh, the whole universe of the moving and the unmoving joined together as one in my body and whatever else you desire to see.
CH 11.7

But since you cannot see Me with these eyes of yours,I give you divine sight; behold My divine power.
CH 11.8

Sanjay said:
Having thus spoken, O King, the great lord of yoga Hari showed to Partha, His supreme godly form.
CH 11.9

If the light of a thousand suns were to blaze forth at once in the sky, that would be like the splendour of that mighty being.
CH 11.12

There in the body of the God of gods, Pandava then beheld the whole universe, in its manifold diversity, drawn together into one.
CH 11.13

Then Dhananjaya, struck with amazement, his hair standing on end, bowed his head in awe and with joined palms, spoke these words.
CH 11.14

Arjun said:
I behold You, infinite in forms on all sides, with countless arms bellies, faces and eyes; but I see in You no end nor middle nor beginning, O Lord of the universe, O Universal Form.
CH 11.16

I see You with diadem, club and discus; a mass of radiance blazing everywhere, hard to look at, dazzling about like fires and suns immeasurable.

CH 11.17

I see You without beginning, middle or end, infinite in power, of infinite arms, the sun and the moon are Your eyes. Your mouth is gleaming fire; Your radiance heats the whole universe.

CH 11:19

This space between heaven and earth and all the quarters are filled by You alone. Having seen all this, Your marvelous and terrible form, the three worlds are trembling with fear, O Great Being.
CH 11.20

The Blessed Lord said:
I am Time, mighty and world annihilating, now engaged in wiping out the world. Even without you the warriors arrayed in confronting ranks shall not live.
CH 11.32

Arjun said:
It is right, O Hrishikesh, that the world is delighted and rejoices in your praise: demons fly in fear in all directions and all the hosts of adepts do homage.
CH 11.36

And why should they not bow to You, O Great -souled One, the Primal Cause even of Brahma, O Infinite Being, O Lord of gods, O abode of the universe; You are the Imperishable, the being and the non-being, that which is Supreme.
CH 11.37

You are the Primal God, the Ancient One; You are the Abode of the universe. You are the Knower and the Known and the ultimate Abode; this universe is pervaded by You, O being of infinite form.
CH 11.38

Whatever I have said from carelessness or love, addressing You as 'O Krishna, O Yadav, O friend', presumptuously, looking upon You merely as a friend, ignorant of this your greatness; In whatever way I may have shown disrespect in jest or at play, reposing, sitting or at meals, whether alone or in company - that I implore

You, Immeasurable One, to forgive.
CH 11.41 / 42

Therefore, bowing down, prostrating my body, I implore You adorable Lord to forgive me. Bear with me, Lord as a father with his son, as a friend with his friend, as a lover with his beloved.
CH 11.44

I rejoice that I have seen what has never been seen before, but my mind is confounded with fear. Show me that form only, O God; have mercy. O God of gods, O Abode of the universe. I desire to see you as before, crowned, bearing a mace and discus in the hand, in Your former guise having four arms, O thousand - armed. O Universal Form.
CH 11.45 / 46

The Blessed Lord said:
Graciously, by my divine power have I shown you, O Arjun, this Supreme form, resplendent, infinite, primeval, which none but you has ever seen.
CH 11.47

Be neither afraid nor bewildered on seeing this terrible form of mine; free from fear and delighted at heart, behold again my former shape.
CH 11.49

Sanjaya said:
Having thus spoken to Arjun, Vasudeva[35] showed again His own form; and the great-souled One assuming His gentle form consoled him who was terrified.
CH 11.50

Arjun said:
Having seen this your gentle human form, O Janardana, I am now composed and am restored to my own nature.
CH 11.51

35 Son of Vasudeva - Krishna.

CHAPTER

12

WORSHIPPING THE MANIFEST AND THE UNMANIFEST AND THE IDEAL MAN

Which is a preferable form of worship - God as unmanifest and without attributes or God as manifest with attributes - Krishna explains that worshipping a formless God is difficult and troublesome for the embodied - The preferable path of worship is of a God with form and attributes - Path of knowledge is superior to ritualistic prayer - Meditation is superior to path of knowledge - Selfless action is superior to meditation - Devotees are however free to follow the path of their choice - Qualities of the ideal man dearest to God.

We have already seen in more than one chapter the unique tolerance and liberality of the Gita towards diverse paths of worship. Indeed, I would not be wrong in claiming that it is this philosophically inclusive approach in his most sacred of religious texts that makes the Hindu inclined to be less dogmatic and tolerant towards different spiritual approaches, than followers of other religions. It also makes him more curious to know the spiritual treasures that may lie elsewhere. Within the Hindu faith the issues of worshipping God as manifest through Avatars, beings, forms or idols, as opposed to worshipping Him as unmanifest, formless, non-being, with no attributes, have been reconciled, recognizing the legitimacy of both paths. This emerges clearly in this chapter.

Arjun poses the crucial question. Which kind of worship is superior, the one who conceives of God as with form and attributes (Sagun Brahma) or the one who conceives of God as unmanifest and without form and attributes (Nirgun Brahma). The Judaic faiths advocate worship of a God who approximates to the unmanifest, characterized by 'Nirgun Brahma'. Though the approximation of course is not complete for the reason that Christianity, Islam and Judaism have a spiritual cosmology which is dualistic, in which the creator and His creation are distinct and separate entities and to confuse one with the other would amount to blasphemy. Thus the great Sufi mystic Hallaj was crucified in Baghdad in the tenth century for claiming, "I am the truth" ('Ana al Haq'), much like the Hindu aphorism "Thou are That" (Tat tvam asi). The Hindu faith is Monist, where the creator and His creation are one and the apparent duality is an illusion to be overcome, whatever path one chooses in worship.

Krishna asserts that it is indeed much more difficult and troublesome to worship and comprehend God as unmanifest, the imperishable, the indefinable, the unthinkable, the unchangeable, the immovable and the eternal, for the simple reason that the worshipper is himself embodied and has a form (Ch.12. 5). Thus being embodied if a person were to worship God with attributes and a form, familiar and comprehensible, that would not only be easier for him but would be a superior form of worship being the more practicable: "Those who....... Worship Me (Sagun Brahma) - them do I consider perfect in Yoga" (Ch. 12. 2).

A corporeal self can learn and advance through corporeality alone. He is a subject and has to have an object. That object has to be palpable and corporeal. Such an object may be a ray of light or a work of art conveying the truth, evolved according to his own culture and tradition. It may be an icon, an Avatar, a saint or a sacred book. Even where iconography is condemned as heathenism we see some sort of symbols cropping up automatically, as by its very nature the mind cannot concentrate on nothingness.

Arjun is then told the techniques by which one may practice the Yoga of worship so that one is able to experience spiritual enlightenment.

Better than ritualistic prayer is knowledge. Standing in a temple with folded hands paying homage, prostrating in routine prayer is

Abhyasa Yoga. Better than this is the understanding that divinity is not confined to temples or to rituals but is much more. Such an appreciation comes from knowing and studying spirituality (path of knowledge). Better than such knowledge is the practice of meditation on divinity. But superior even to meditation is acting selflessly to achieve noble ends in the service of God. There are many stages and paths for the devout; routine prayer, introspection, meditation and best of all, selfless action for noble ends. However, let the devotee do whatever he can as all is acceptable.

Finally Arjun is told in the most heart moving verses, of the kind of person who is dearest before God, the ideal man. Some time back I sent these verses to a foreign friend. She was so moved that she included them in her annual New Year greeting card so that all her friends could have a chance of reading what had impressed her so much.

Krishna tells Arjun that His favourite devotee would be one who has the following qualities:

One, who hates no being, is friendly and compassionate towards all. One, who is not arrogant and covetous, even minded in pain and pleasure and forgiving.

One, who is content, given to meditation, is self controlled and firm in resolve, with mind and intellect dedicated to God's purpose. One who does not agitate others nor is agitated by the world. One who is not touched by envy, fear and anxiety nor overwhelmed by joy.

One who is free from cravings, pure, dexterous and expert in what he does, unaffected by circumstances, adverse or favourable, and untroubled and selfless in all his undertakings. One who neither rejoices nor hates, neither grieves nor becomes the slave of his desires. One who renouncing good and evil (non judgmental), full of devotion, such a person is dear to me (ch.12, 13 -20)

Mahatma Gandhi who was a follower of the Gita's precepts quickly comes to ones mind when one thinks of the qualities which make a devotee God's favourite.

BHAKTI YOGA
(Excerpts)

Arjun said:
Those devotees who, ever steadfast, worship you thus and those again who worsip the Imperishable, the unmanifest - which of these best follow the Rule?
CH 12.1

The blessed Lord said:
Those who, fixing their minds on me, worship me with perpetual devotion, endowed with supreme faith - them do I consider most perfect in the Rule.
CH 12.2

But those who worship the Imperishable, the Indefinable, the Unmanifested, the Omnipresent, the Unthinkable, the Unchangable, the, Immovable, the Eternal; having restrained all their senses, even minded everywhere, rejoicing in the welfare of all beings - win to Me also.
CH 12.4

Greater is their difficulty whose minds are set on the Unmanifested, for the goal of the Unmanifested is very hard for the embodied to reach.
CH 12.5

Better indeed is knowledge than ritual practice; better than knowledge is meditation; better than meditation is the surrender of the fruits of action; peace immediately follows renunciation.
CH 12.12

He who hates no being, who is friendly and compassionate to all, who is free from the feeling of 'I' and 'mine', even-minded in pain and pleasure and forgiving; ever content, steady in meditation, with mind and intellect fixed on me, he my devotee is dear to me.
CH 12.13 / 14

He by whom the world is not afflicted and whom the world cannot afflict, he who is not overwhelmed by joy, free of anger, fear and anxiety - he is dear to me.
CH 12.15

He who has no wants, who is pure, skillful, impartial, untroubled and who is selfless in all his undertakings, he who is thus devoted to me, is dear to me.
CH 12.16

He who neither rejoices nor hates nor grieves nor desires, who renounces alike fair and foul, full of devotion, he is dear to me.
CH 12.17

He who is the same to friend and foe and also in honour and dishonour, who is the same in cold and heat, in pleasure and pain, who is free from attachment; who is neither moved by censure or praise, who is silent, content with whatever comes his way, homeless, steady-minded full of devotion - that man is dear to me.
CH 12.18 / 19

CHAPTER

13

THE FIELD AND THE KNOWER OF THE FIELD

The 'Field' is the body, the 'Knower of the Field' is the Soul - The Field is also nature and its elements, the Knower is the divine essence imbuing it - What is Knowledge and what ignorance - What is worth knowing is the Absolute Unmanifest, 'Nirguna Brahma', though it remains paradoxical and inconceivable - Gross matter becomes dynamic in the presence of God's radiant essence - Agitated nature then spins physical and subtle sheaths around the Soul, captivating it - The sheaths ultimately dissolve as the personality evolves overcoming the ego.

In this chapter we return to the nature of the corporeal personality and its indweller. The body is the result of nature (Prakriti) and its inhabitant (Purush) is the soul, also termed the field (Kshetra) and the knower of the field (Kshetragya)

Krishna explains that the corporeal personality is the field of action around which life plays its events. The knower of the field is the soul; the conscience and the intuitive understanding that arise from it. Krishna says that He is the knower of the field in all 'fields' of being.

The field consists of the five elements, fire, air, water, earth and ether; the senses of knowledge (Gyan Indriya) such as the eye, ear, skin, tongue and nose; the five organs of action (Karma Indriya) such as the hand, foot, mouth, anus and the genital organs. The field is characterized by desire, hatred, pleasure, pain, intelligence and egoism, the total living organism.

Arjun wishes to know what knowledge (Gyan) is and what ignorance. Krishna replies that qualities such as humility, modesty, non-violence, forbearance, uprightness, service to the teacher, purity, steadfastness, self control, dispassion towards objects of the senses, absence of egoism, the understanding that birth, death, old age, sickness, and pain are the inevitable products of living, constant effort at gaining self knowledge, unswerving devotion to Him and believing that one is not separate, constitute knowledge and the absence of these is ignorance.

Arjun also wants to know what is it that ought to be known (Gneyam). Krishna explains that one attains to immortality when one knows the nature of the Absolute Unmanifest (Nirgun Brahma). It is without beginning and is neither being nor non-being. It is omnipresent and all enveloping. It shines forth as energy in the senses, though it is without senses itself. It is absolute and all sustaining. It has no natural attributes (Gunas), yet experiences them all. It is around and within all beings, moving everywhere and yet in a sense immovable. It is apparently far and yet near. It is undivided and yet appears to be divided in beings. It dissolves and generates. It is the light of all lights. On account of its subtlety, which at times appears to be contradictory to the ordinary mind it remains incomprehensible.

He then goes on to explain that the body and the senses are produced by nature (Prakriti). Purush is the innermost consciousness which is itself a particle of the universal conscience, the guiding force and sustainer of Prakriti. The Purush is impervious to the activities of Prakriti but the ego (Ahankar) experiences the genetic traits (Gunas) born of Prakriti and begins to identify with them.

Prakriti is basically gross matter without character or shape when the Gunas are in balance. With such a balance there is only inert matter. But the mere presence of Purush, the radiant essence, makes the Gunas agitated, illuminated and excited and air, ether, fire, water, and earth are created from the stirring combinations of Gunas. The more the agitation the more substantial and diverse creation gets with the increase of the basest traits, the 'Tamsik Guna'.

We may recall that Krishna said earlier:

"Animating My Prakriti, I send forth again and again all the multitude of beings, helpless under the regime of My Prakriti" (Ch. 9, 8).

"Because of My proximity, Prakriti produces all this, the moving and the un-moving; the world thus revolves....." (Ch.9, 10).

Thus the Universal Purush, the cosmic essence, by its radiant presence unleashes creation in inert matter and Purush as the individual soul, Atma, in proxmity with Prakriti results in it stirring to form enveloping layers, gross and subtle round its radiant nucleus. When enlightenment dawns on the 'personality', which is a specific combination of Gunas in the individual entity, these layers gradually lose the Gunas, until finally they dissolve and the Purush within is now pure Atma, the divine spark, which merges, thus released, with the supreme essence, Paramatma.

Both Purush and Prakriti are eternal. The phenomenal world as we noted is produced by the interaction of the Divine Essence with nature. That essence can be realized through deep concentration and meditation. Some may merely be able to understand its virtues. But the one who gets deeply rooted to his inner self (Antaryami) gets conjoined with the eternal flux of things. For such a person the 'Knower of the Field' of life and bodily actions becomes the ever present guide. Those who can thus assimilate the knowledge of the physical 'Field' and its 'Knower', the generator, arrive at the truth of the matter and their actions then automatically become rightful action. This understanding can dawn through meditation, seeking after knowledge or through rightful selfless action. Still others grasp this truth through worship and listening to the discourses of sages and Gurus.

The interaction of the 'Field' and the 'Knower' creates the living universe. The supreme essence is the same everywhere and all beings rest in the one Supreme Self (Paramatma). It has no beginning and possesses no physical traits. It dwells in the body yet neither acts nor is tainted by action. Thus one has to understand the distinction between the 'Field' and the 'Knower' of the Field.

KSHETRA KSHETRAGYA VIBHAGA YOGA (Excerpts)

The Blessed Lord said:

This body, O Kaunteya[36], is called the Kshetra, the field; he who knows it is called Kshetragya by the sages.

CH 13.1

And know Me as the Kshetragya in all Kshetras. O Bharata. The knowledge of Kshetra and Kshetragya is considered by Me as true knowledge.

CH 13.2

The great elements, ego, intellect, the unmanifest, the ten senses and the one mind and the five objects of the senses;

Desire, hatred, pleasure, pain, the bodily whole, intelligence, firmness - these are said to summarize the Kshetra with its modifications.

CH 13.5 / 6

Constancy in Self - knowledge, perception of the knowledge of Truth; this is declared to be knowledge and what is opposed to it is ignorance.

CH 13.11

Now will I descrbe that which is to be known, by knowing which one partakes of immortality - the beginning less supreme Brahman, which is neither Being nor Non-Being.

CH 13.12

With hands and feet everywhere, with eyes and hands and mouths everywhere, with ears everywhere - He exists enveloping all.

Shining through the functions of the senses, yet without the senses; Unattached yet sustaining all; devoid of Gunas, yet He experiences them.

Without and within all beings; the unmoving and also the moving; because of His subtlety He is incomprehensible; He is far and near.

CH 13.13 / 14 / 15

He is undivided and yet He seems divided in beings. He is to be known as the supporter of beings. He devours and He generates.

CH 13.1 6

In the production of the body and the senses, Prakriti is said to be the cause; in the experience of pleasure and pain, Purush is said to be the cause.

CH 13.20

---

36 Son of Kunti - Arjun

Purush seated in Prakriti, experiences the Gunas born of Prakriti; attachment to the Gunas is the cause of his birth in good and evil wombs.
CH 13.21

The Supreme Purush in this body is also called the Witness, the Sanctioner, the Sustainer, the One who experiences, the Great Lord and the Supreme self.
CH 13.22

Whatever being is born, the unmoving or the moving, O best of Bharatas, know it to be from the union of Kshetra and Kshetragya.
CH 13. 26

He sees, who sees the Supreme Lord, remaining the same in all beings, the imperishable in the perishable.
CH 13.27

He truly sees, who sees that all actions are done by Prakriti alone and the Atma is action less.
CH 13.29

Having no beginning and possessing no Gunas, the Supreme Self, imperishable, though dwelling in the body, O Kaunteya, neither acts nor is tainted.
CH 13.31

They who perceive with the eye of wisdom this distinction between the Kshetra and the Kshetragya and the deliverance of beings from Prakriti, they go to the supreme.
CH 13.34

CHAPTER

14

THE THREE NATURAL TRAITS

The Sattva Guna, quality of clarity binds the soul to a personality given to righteousness - The Rajas Guna, quality of passion and dynamism attaches the soul to an active and sensual personality - The Tamas Guna, quality of ignorance and delusion binds the soul to a personality given to indolence and indiscretion - The three traits (Gunas) in nature combine in beings and objects in varying degrees - A balanced, calm and wise personality rising above the Gunas frees the soul from rebirth - Concept of Soul is central to philosophy of the Gita - If the Soul is not agent of action how does it influence the personality it inhabits - Implication is that it does so through inspiration and intuition which may or may not be heeded - If heeded there is evolution to liberation - If not the cycle of indefinite re-births continues - Why do embodied Souls charter diverse courses through re-births when they are equal reflections of the Divine Essence - Creation is Maya, illusory, and a play, Leela, for the Omniscient One.

The universal essence has the attributes of both male and female. The first attribute is that of a great womb in which it places its cosmic seed resulting in the birth of all beings. The great womb is God as nature (Prakriti) and as the provider of seed, God is the father.

We have learnt earlier that the physical world is characterized by three Gunas (traits) of nature in varying combinations in beings, objects and forces. When after its inception, in the course of timelessness the universe multiplied its objectivity, the three aspects of temperament got ingrained in nature. This is the basic temperament of the universe and creation. This naturally trickled down into the personality of all beings.

The Atma gets embodied and fettered in the body on account of the interaction of the three traits in nature. The Sattva Guna, the quality of clarity, being luminous, stainless and pure, binds the soul to the body creating attachment to righteousness and knowledge. The Rajas Guna being inclined to passion and dynamism attaches the soul to an active and sensual body. The Tamas Guna which is characterized by ignorance and delusion binds the soul to a body given to indiscretion, indolence and sleep. The three traits combine in differing proportions in different individuals producing diverse effects of bondage for the soul. The predominance of the first makes one a luminous personality, that of the second, one that is restless, sensual and prone to intense activity, whereas the third makes a person indiscreet, slothful, careless and confused. Thus at death when Sattva predominates one may rise to heavenly planes, when Rajas, one is reborn in an active environment and when Tamas holds sway, one is born in an environment of confusion, delusion and ignorance.

However, once a soul has succeeded in overcoming the three Gunas it is freed from rebirth and resumes its blissful immortality. To achieve this one has to be balanced, calm, unaffected by circumstances, agreeable or disagreeable, to be the same in praise and censure, honour and dishonour. One who being aware of the play of the Gunas in nature, rises above them, that person's soul returns to its disembodied state of immortality and is not reborn.

The nature of a person who has overcome the Gunas is far from clear to Arjun and he proceeds to ask - 'what are the marks that distinguish such a person... how does he behave... how does he rise above them?'

The one who has 'crossed over' the Gunas, views the storms they create with equanimity and composure and without judgment. Raw nature after all is both spectacular and fearsome in its ruthlessness. The predators will kill to eat, the prey will seek to escape, lust and passion will remain a predominant force in procreation, anger and vengeance will result in murder and mayhem, jealousy and greed will produce crime, slothfulness and lethargy will result in procrastination and indiscretion, even as love and maternity will produce compassion and devotion and sacrifice, rare altruistic behaviour - different combinations of Gunas at work.

Krishna explains that such a person neither hates the Gunas nor is attached to them: 'sitting like one unconcerned, is moved not by the Gunas, knowing that they operate, but himself remains firm and moves not', comes the complex and subtle reply. Nothing moves him anymore; he is beyond earthly cares, already a part of eternal and absolute bliss.

Central to the philosophy of the Gita is the concept of the Soul. The Soul is the divine spark in the body and is repeatedly called the embodied one and the indweller. It is a part or reflection (Ansha) of the Super-Soul, the divine force, the Supreme Essence. While the concept is introduced in chapter two, it remains a recurrent theme for discussion and explanation throughout the Gita.

The Soul as the indweller and embodied divine essence is also said to reincarnate time and again through rebirth. Chapter thirteen and fourteen in particular focus on this process of the Soul's journey till it finally is free of the material fetters and merges back into its original essence, the Super-Soul. Chapter thirteen explains how Nature becomes aroused and agitated in the presence of the divine essence and seeks to envelop it, thus causing embodiment of souls. Chapter fourteen finally dwells more thoroughly on the manner in which diverse aspects of Nature or gross matter become agitated, producing forces with specific qualities - luminosity and truth, fiery passion, sensuality and furious activity and third, indolence, lethargy and ignorance. These forces thus agitated materialize and envelop souls in varying degrees, dragging them through the material experiences of life, marking and scarring the subtle body covering it with karmic effects which thereafter determine the course it will charter in future reincarnations.

It is reiterated from chapter to chapter that the agent of action is not the soul but the combination of the three Gunas acting independently through the body, the ego and the personality. When this complexity of the 'non-acting soul' and the acting body and ego finally succeed in overcoming the Karmic effects of many life times, through deep introspection and selfless action, then the soul wins release.

However it is never clearly explained how the 'non-acting soul' is able to achieve this feat. One can only infer that the soul being part of the divine essence continuously radiates inspiration and intuition which produce all the great altruistic marvels of mortal man. This constant inner-voice may be heeded as the voice of one's conscience by the gross body and its personality, helping it to turn the forces of inertia and ignorance (Tamas) into the superior force of passionate action (Rajas) and to evolve to the force of luminosity and clarity (Sattva). Eventually the inner voice would help the gross body- personality to go beyond even luminosity to the ultimate state of complete liberation. These prodding's by the in-dweller when not heeded leave the complexity of 'non-acting soul' and acting gross body-personality in a static situation, impelling re-birth ad infinitum-through some eight million wombs according to the scriptures (Chaurasi Lakh Yoni).

Again it is not clear how a particular soul in the first instance gets enveloped with a certain combination of Gunas and why. If we were to apply logic then all souls must be subjected to equal proportions of the three traits. But then why is it that some embodied souls evolve faster than others? This remains a mystery since all souls are equal reflections of the divine essence, none superior and none inferior. This calls for further introspection.

Well we can conjecture that this is because the Divine Essence wishes to sample material existence in all its facets - luminous, passionate and indolent to comprehend and experience the infinite range of its own Nature. It thus allows its fragment souls to be enveloped by different proportions of the Guna traits, randomly, to achieve an unlimited and diverse range of possibilities. This is only conjecture and there are no clear answers.

Here the Gita's description of Brahman, the Divine Essence, comes to mind. With hands and feet everywhere, with eyes and ears and mouths everywhere - He exists enveloping all, devoid of the Gunas, yet He experiences them. Neither Being nor Non-Being, far and yet near, undivided and yet appearing divided in beings, shining through the functions of the senses, yet without senses. He remains the same in all beings - because of His subtlety He is incomprehensible (Ch.13.13/16) . In physics too when one moves from the Newtonian world of material certainties to the Quantum uncertainties of the microcosmic world, we are confronted by similar mind blowing ambiguities and paradoxes which appear incomprehensible.

As Arjun aptly asserts in chapter ten -"only You alone know Yourself by Yourself". As in Zen meditations, with the 'little mind' one can analyze indefinitely but with the 'big mind' subtle comprehension can dawn in silence. The word 'Maya', illusion, is appropriate. The whole experience of Creation is just a play (Leela) for the One who is after all omniscient, all knowing and really needs no experience to know any more.

GUNATRAYA VIBHAGA YOGA
(Excerpts)

The Blessed Lord said:
My womb is the Great Brahma (Prakriti); in that I place the seed; thence, O Bharata, spring all beings.
CH 14.3

Whatever forms are produced, O Kaunteya, in any wombs whatsoever, the great Brahma is their womb, I the seed - giving Father.
CH 14.4

Sattva, Rajas, Tamas - these Gunas, O mighty-armed, born of Prakriti, bind the indestructible embodied one fast in the body.
CH 14.5

Of these, Sattva, being luminous and untroubled, binds by creating attachment to happiness and attachment to knowledge, O sinless one.
CH 14.6

Know Rajas to be of the nature of passion, the source of yearning and attachment; it fetters, O Kaunteya, the embodied one by attachment to action.
CH 14.7

But know Tamas to be born of ignorance, deluding all embodied beings; it fetters, O Bharata, by heedlessness, indolence and sleep.
CH 14.8

If the embodied one faces dissolution when Sattva is predominant, then he goes to the pure world of the most exalted knowers.
CH 14.14

Facing dissolution in Rajas, he is born among those attached to action; and dying in Tamas, he is born in the wombs of the deluded.
CH 14.15

When the beholder perceives that there is no agent of action other than the Gunas and knows Him who is higher than the Gunas, he enters into My Being.
CH 14.19

The embodied one having crossed over these three Gunas out of which the body is evolved, is freed from birth, death, decay and pain and attains to immortality.
CH 14.20

Arjun said:
What are the marks, O Lord, of him who has crossed over the three Gunas? What is his conduct? And how does he rise above the Gunas?
CH 14.21

The Blessed Lord said:
He, O Pandava, who hates not light, activity and delusion, when present, nor craves for them when absent;

He who as one sitting unconcerned, is not shaken by the Gunas, who stands unaffected, knowing it is but the Gunas that move;

CH 14.22 / 23

Balanced in pleasure and pain, self-possessed, viewing a clod of earth, a stone and gold alike; the same towards the agreeable and the disagreeable, firm, the same in censure and praise;

The same in honour and dishonour, the same to friend and foe, renouncing all undertakings - he is said to have risen above the Gunas.
CH 14.24 / 25

CHAPTER

15

THE TREE OF LIFE

The Banyan tree shows the relationship between the physical and the spiritual - The Tree of Life can be cut by the axe of non-attachment - The experiences of life imprinted on the Atma create a new personality at rebirth - Explanation of Purushottam - The tree of life and Purushottam.

In India the Banyan tree (Peepal) has a special significance for showing the relationship between the physical and the spiritual. It is a tree with roots descending from branches above. In a sense it is the image of a cosmic tree with spiritual roots above and its life force developing into branches, leaves and sensual buds in the material world it has spawned below. In this chapter the Gita employs the symbolism of such a tree, called by Krishna the Ashvatha tree. Ashvatha means that which is not today what it was yesterday, ever changing, impermanent and unstable. This is phenomenal existence, which is neither constant nor steady. It originates in the roots of Brahma from above and as its branches descend they get more and more material, diverse and sensual. Prakriti branches down from its source the Super-Soul (Paramatma).

For salvation this tree has to be cut asunder by the axe of non-attachment. This is possible for those who with perfect self-discipline turn indifferent to doting love (Moha) and other worldly attachments (Sanga Dosh), relying on a perfect spiritual discipline.

When a soul leaves the body it takes with its subtle body all experiences acquired in life. Not unlike the brain which receives impressions and proceeds to analyze and store it in deep memory, I believe that the Atma when it leaves the body takes the finer cumulated impressions and ideas of this life and previous lives in its electro-magnetic complexity, the subtle body and these again rear their head after a lapse of time, possibly centuries, in a new birth with a new personality. While the Atma is not material these impressions become a new material personality. Those who have lived a straight and good life of constant introspection on the inner self are born into fortunate circumstances. The chapter on Purushottam Yoga is rather mysterious in its connotations.

Krishna concludes the chapter with an explanation of the term Purushottam, which can be translated to mean the Supreme Indweller. A part (Ansha) of the Supreme Essence (Brahma) becomes the timeless soul in the living world attracting to itself the five senses and the mind. Thus He experiences the senses and when He leaves the body He carries the flavour of the sensual experience with Him. While here, He readily mingles with the Gunas, the individual's traits. His subtle glow is within all beings. Furthermore He also energizes and sustains the world through the light of the sun, the moon and fire. Thus there is in the world, the perishable, our bodies and the imperishable, the soul but beyond both there is a third, the Supreme Self, Purushottam, the one who inhabits the individual while pervading and supporting the world.

To the superficial reader, the two halves of the chapter would appear unconnected. After a little pondering however, the connection suddenly dawns as the chapter concludes. The question arises, what has the analogy of the Ashvatha tree to do with Purushottam? Well, as the spiritual sap of the Ashvatha tree descends through its roots hanging from above to the branches, leaves and sensual buds in the material world below, so too a part of Purushottam, the Ansha descends into beings and merges with their senses and traits and moods and again through the light of the sun, moon and fire enlivens them. When with the axe of detachment the tree is cut asunder, it departs again with all the flavours and aromas that it created.

The purpose of the analogy and the essential message of the discourse is to underline that one must be aware at all times of the ubiquitous and palpable presence of divinity which alone gives meaning to life and living, senses and sensuality and the material and phenomenal world, from within and without.

PURUSHOTTAM YOGA
(Excerpts)

The Blessed Lord said:

They speak of an imperishable Ashvattha tree with its roots above and branches below. Its leaves are the Psalms; he who knows it is the knower of the Vedas.
CH 15.1

Below and above spread its branches, nourished by the Gunas; sense-objects are its buds; and below in the world of men stretch forth the roots, engendering action.
CH 15.2

Its form is not perceived here as such, neither its end, nor its origin, nor its source. Having cut asunder this firm rooted Ashvattha with the strong axe of non attachment;

Then that Goal must be sought, going wither, they do not return again. I seek refuge in that Primeval Purush whence streamed forth the ancient cosmic energy.
CH 15.3 / 4

An eternal portion of Myself having become the eternal soul in the living world, draws to itself Nature's five senses and the mind.

When this Sovereign-Soul which has been in the body, leaves, he takes these along, as the wind carries the scent from their sources.

Presiding over hearing, sight, touch, taste, smell, and mind, he experiences sense objects.
CH 15.7 / 8 / 9

Whether he departs, or stays, or experiences, the deluded do not see, only those who possess the eye of wisdom do.
CH 15.10

There are two kinds of beings in the world the perishable and the imperishable. The perishable is the living being and the imperishable is the Self.
CH 15.16

But there is another and higher being, called the Supreme Self, the immutable Lord who pervades and sustains the three worlds.
CH 15.17

As I transcend the perishable and am above even the imperishable, therefore am I known in the world and in the Vedas as 'Purushottam', the highest Purush.
CH 15.18

CHAPTER

16

DIVINE AND DEMONIC NATURES

Divine and demonic traits in men - those with a demonic nature hate the divinity within them and in others - Hypocrisy is particularly condemnable.

Certain qualities are divine while others are demonic. Those with divine qualities become liberated, whereas the ones with demonic traits fall and are reborn in 'demonic wombs' in conditions lower than before.

Divine qualities are fearlessness, purity of heart, commitment to knowledge and Yoga, charity, control of the senses, dedicated action, study of scriptures, austerity and straightforwardness, truth, non-violence, absence of anger, serenity, absence of crookedness, compassion, lack of greed, gentleness, modesty, absence of fickleness, vigour, forgiveness, fortitude, absence of hatred and pride.

Demonic traits are ostentation, arrogance, conceit, harshness, ignorance, lack of discretion and falsehood. People with such traits have little faith in God, no belief in a moral basis for creation or in the physical world having been created by a higher order. With such a world view they are possessed of insatiable desires and are proud, arrogant and hypocritical. Their world view being deviated they act with impure resolve. They are driven by lust and anger and strive to secure wealth and sensual enjoyment through unjust means. They are possessive, acquisitive, violent and stubborn and believe themselves to be superior, powerful and happy. They pride themselves over their riches and high status in society and are ostentatious. When they engage in charity and rituals, it is from a standpoint of ignorance and to obtain material gains.

Many would fall in this category from kings to hypocritical sages. Ravan the great adversarial figure of the Ramayana was proud, arrogant, unreasonable, stubborn, acquisitive, violent, crude and thoroughly immoral. His prayers and sacrifices were tainted as they were made with ulterior motives to empower himself rather than for true spiritual emancipation. Likewise in the present day we come across some godmen who manipulate and exploit their disciples for acquiring wealth and power and even to satisfy their carnal desires. Some powerful political leaders like Hitler do the same causing the destruction of social and humanitarian norms in the name of false and wicked ideologies. There are numerous economic offences committed by high and low, pretending that their actions benefit everybody.

The Gita talks not merely of the good and bad but very emphatically about hypocritical activity posing as altruism but in fact being totally exploitative and evil. This last category the Gita considers particularly condemnable. The three gateways to hell are lust, anger and greed. Krishna tells Arjun that such people hate the divinity within them and the divinity in others. He closes the discourse by assuring Arjun that he need not worry for his nature is divine.

DAIVASURA SAMPAD VIBHAG YOGA (Excerpts)

The Blessed Lord said:

Fearlessness, purity of heart, staedfastness in knowledge and yoga, almsgiving, control of the senses, sacrifice, study of the scriptures, austerity and straightforwardness;

Non-violence, truth, freedom from anger, renunciation, serenity, absence of crookedness, compassion for beings, freedom from greed, gentleness, modesty, absence of fickleness;

Vigour, forgiveness, fortitude, purity, absence of hatred, absence of pride, these belong to one born for a divine state, O Bharata.

CH 16.1/ 2/ 3

Hypocrisy, arrogance and self conceit, wrath and rudeness and ignorance belong to one who is born, O Partha, for a demonic state.

CH 16.4

The divine nature leads to liberation, the demonic to bondage; grieve not, O Pandava, you are born for a divine state.
CH 16.5

The demonic know not what to do and what to refrain from; neither purity, nor right conduct nor truth is found in them.
CH 16.7

They say, the universe is without intention, without a moral basis, without a God, born of mutual union, brought about by lust; what else?
CH 16.8

Bound by a hundred ties of hope, given over to anger, they strive to secure by unjust means hoards of wealth for sensual enjoyment.
CH 16.12

Bewildered by many a fancy, enmeshed in the snare of delusion, addicted to the gratification of lust, they fall into a foul hell.
CH 16.16

Given over to egoism, power, pride, desire and wrath, these malicious people hate Me in their own bodies and those of others.
CH 16.18

Triple are the gates of hell, destructive of the self - lust, anger, and greed; therefore should one forsake these three.
CH 16.21

The man who is liberated from these three gates to darkness, O Kaunteya, practices what is good for him and thus goes to the Supreme Good.
CH 16.22

CHAPTER

17

THE FAITHFUL AND THE MISGUIDED

Three types of nature in matters of faith, austerities, preferred cuisines, sacrifices, charities and gifts - Violent and tortuous austerities condemned - Sacrifices, donations and austerities are of no avail without faith.

In this chapter Krishna dwells on the behaviour of the three types of people, mainly in matters of faith - those predominantly good and truthful, those swayed by a passionate and arrogant nature and those in the thrall of indolence, apathy and ignorance. If you believe in rebirth, as Hindus, Buddhists and Jains do then intrinsic nature cannot be attributed merely to genetics but to an antecedent and ulterior Karmic source. How this unfolds when confronted by environment, education and circumstances is governed by intrinsic nature powered by the Gunas. However this is not entirely deterministic as room is allowed for evolution and while the tendency is there it can be overcome either in a positive direction or a negative one. Thus a saint can devolve into a sinner and vice versa.

Krishna describes how these three basic natures unfold in engaging in physical and spiritual activity. He touches upon the differing forms of worship and faith, austerities, preferred cuisines, sacrifices, charity and gifts.

The pure and good at heart worship luminous, benign gods, sages and teachers. Their faith is strong and their spiritual practices are aimed at enlightenment and not for achievement of earthly objectives. Their food is pure, a source of health and vigour, savoury, substantial and agreeable, producing joy and cheerfulness. Their sacrifices are performed without desiring fruit, out of a sense of duty. Their speech is truthful, pleasant and beneficial, their minds are serene, gentle and controlled, their charity is made towards people incapable of returning favours, at the right time and place and to those who are truly worthy of receiving it.

Those possessed of a proud, arrogant, conceited and passionate nature, worship wrathful and fiery demonic entities. Their austerities are violent. They torture the body with egoistical and hypocritical motives, impelled by lust and desire for material gain and empowerment. This is doubtless a reference to painful austerities practiced in India, like sleeping on a bed of iron nails, piercing body parts, self flagellation, walking on fire, standing on one leg indefinitely and staring at the sun etc. Krishna bluntly dismisses these practices with the words:

" They are fools, who torture their bodily organs and Me too who dwells within the body....know that their resolve is demonic." (Ch.17, 6)

Their austerities are performed with ostentation to gain respect, honour and praise and the results are naturally unstable and transitory. Furthermore their craving is for foods that are bitter, sour, over spiced, pungent, saline, dry and burning, producing pain, unhappiness and disease. Their sacrifices are performed with ulterior motives of reward or self glorification and empowerment. The charity they perform is in the hope of receiving rewards in the hereafter. The gifts they present are with a view to receive gifts in return and this is also done reluctantly.

The lowest category, the ignorant, slothful, apathetic natures, worship ghosts and nature spirits. They enjoy eating food that is impure, that has gone stale or putrid full of maggots, food that stinks or is tasteless. Their sacrifices are not in accordance with any scriptures, bereft of chanting sacred verses, devoid of true faith and which is not accompanied by distribution of food and alms. Their austerities are practiced with foolish obstinacy, with self torture and with the goal not of enlightenment or even for profit but for hurting or destroying others. This brings to mind nefarious practices of worship at cremation grounds or places of burial or other ghoulish activity involving human and infant sacrifice for achieving impossible ends. Their gifts are given at a wrong place or time to unworthy persons, without respect or with insult.

Krishna then pronounces the final word on all such deviated and degrading practices:

" Whatever is sacrificed, given or performed and whatever austerity is practiced without (true) faith, is called Asat (false) and is of no account here or hereafter." (Ch. 17, 28)

SHRADDHATRAYA VIBHAGA YOGA
(Excerpts)

The Blessed Lord said:
The faith of every man, O Bharata, is in accordance with his inherent nature. Man is of the nature of his faith; what his faith is, that indeed he is.
CH 17.3

Sattvik men worship the gods; Rajsik, the demigods and demons; the others - the Tamsik men - the spirits of the dead and ghosts and nature spirits.
CH 17.4

Those men who practice grim mortifications not ordained by the scriptures, conceited and hypocritical, impelled by the force of lust and attachments,

Fools that they are, they torture their bodily organs and Me too, who dwells within the body - know that they are demonic in their resolve.
CH 17.5 / 6

The Foods that augment vitality, energy, vigour, health, joy and cheerfulness, which are savoury are liked by the Sattvik.
CH 17.8

The foods that are bitter, sour, saline, over- hot, pungent, dry and burning are liked by the Rajasik and are productive of pain, grief and disease.
CH 17.9

That which is stale, tasteless, stinking, cooked overnight, refuse and impure is the food liked by the Tamsik.
CH 17.10

That sacrifice is Sattvik which is performed by men desiring no fruit, as enjoined by ordinance, with their mind fixed on the Yagya only, for its own sake.
CH 17.11

That which is performed, O best of the Bharatas, in expectation of a reward or for self-glorification, know that to be a Rajasik sacrifice.
CH 17.12

They declare that sacrifice to be Tamasik which is contrary to the ordinances, in which no food is distributed, no hymns are chanted, no gifts given; such sacrifice is without faith.
CH 17.13

Serenity of the mind, pleasantness, silence, self control and a clean disposition - this is called mental austerity.
CH 17.16

This threefold austerity practiced by steadfast men with the utmost faith, desiring no fruit, they call Sattvik.
CH 17.17

The austerity which is practiced with the object of gaining respect, honour and reverence and with ostentation is said to be Rajasik; it is unstable and transitory.
CH 17.18

That austerity which is practiced with a foolish obstinacy, with self-tortures or for the purpose of destroying another, is declared to be Tamasik.
CH 17.19

That gift which is made to one who can make no return, with a feeling that it is one's duty to give and which is given at the right place and time and to a worthy person, that gift is said to be Sattvik.
CH 17.20

And that gift which is given with a view to receive in return or looking for the fruit or again grudgingly, is considered as Rajasik.
CH 17.21

The gift that is given at a wrong place or time, to unworthy persons, without respect or with insult, that is declared to be Tamasik.
CH 17.22

Whatever is sacrificed, given or performed and whatever austerity is practiced without faith, it is called Asat (false), O Partha, and is worthless both here and in the hereafter.
CH 17.28

CHAPTER

18

THE FINAL WORD

The dialogues having begun with Arjun's argument in favour of relinquishing war, now therefore conclude with examination of issues of renunciation and abandonment at length - Krishna recounts diverse views held by thinkers - definitively rejects misguided abandonment of worthy activities like sacrifice, charity and engaging in austerities - Reiteration that action to be undertaken with detachment not seeking fruit or reward - No forsaking of obligatory duties essential for physical well being or discharging responsibility toward family - The soul is not agent of action - The personality and ego are the agent - concept of 'Daivam' - dispassionate action does not lead to Karmic binding - Three types of persons engaged in action - The four castes - Enlightenment possible for all irrespective of caste, profession and gender - Arjun acknowledges that his delusion and doubt have been finally dispelled - Sanjay hails the dialogues of the Gita.

Krishna returns in his final discourse to the issue of renunciation (Sanyas) and abandonment (Tyag). It is important to recall what caused him in the first place as Arjun's charioteer to halt the battle ready chariot with the two armies arrayed on either side and to launch a series of discourses urging him to fight. It was Arjun's sudden confusion, dismay and despondency and his casting away his weapons with the words 'I will not fight', an act apparently of renunciation and abandonment that instigated Krishna to propound the philosophy of the Gita.

It is for this reason that in the last chapter the discourse returns to this issue of action and the need to clarify to Arjun that one cannot glorify inaction by calling it renunciation, euphemistically.

Despite all the enlightened advice received earlier, Arjun again opens with the seemingly innocuous question - what is the essence of renunciation, abandonment and forsaking. Doubtless what he has in mind is the thought that even now giving up the fight might be considered renunciation. Krishna first recounts various views held by sages and intellectuals. Some say, he recounts, that forsaking the pursuit of health, wealth, domestic life, progeny, name and fame, title and social status (Kamya Karma) is renunciation. Some say abandonment relates to abandoning the desire for fruits of action. Yet others hold that indeed all action should be renounced as evil, while still others declare that one should even give up ritual and sacrificial worship, giving of alms and charity and austerity.

Krishna then pronounces the final judgment. Sacrifices (ritual), charity and austerity should never be given up because they are purifying. However, noble actions should be undertaken with altruism and detachment as to the 'fruits' thereof. Sacrifices should be made for its sake and not for rewards. One should be charitable without hoping to reap returns in the hereafter. Austerity must be undertaken without ulterior motives (Ravan's austerities were for empowerment to gain ascendancy). Relentlessly Krishna moves on to extinguish the last remnants of resistance in Arjun. He makes clear beyond doubt that abandonment of obligatory duties is wrong and such forsaking arises from ignorance. By obligatory duty is meant the actions which help in keeping the organism alive and well. Thus breathing, eating, bathing, exercising, earning wealth, are all basic and mandatory. For the more spiritually evolved it includes ritual sacrifices, charity and austerity. Obligatory duties can also be interpreted to mean duties towards one's family, society and nation. There can be no abandonment of these. That would be a joke of a renunciation.

Krishna stresses that if one does not act, fearing the outcome or from apprehension that the process would be challenging and painful, then such a person is bound to fail in his endeavours. The ideal person is one who engages in obligatory activity with understanding and without doubt, abandoning attachment, neither shrinking from work that is disagreeable nor with obsessive attachment to work that is agreeable. It is clear that Krishna has penetrated the psychology of Arjun where doubt still lingers and the reluctance to fight his kinsmen arises from the extreme unpleasantness of the task. He is confronting Arjun's dilemma head on when he adds further that it is impossible for the embodied to renounce action entirely, therefore there can be no case for such misguided renunciation which some sages or practitioners endorse.

Action is further qualified to mean not merely those of the body but of speech and the mind as well. Time and again it has been clarified in the Gita that the soul (Atma) does not act and only the ignorant believe that it does. Neither the soul nor its original essence the Super-Soul acts through the actions of man; it is nature that does this. The soul remains unmoved and unaffected by Karma. The actor or agent is not the soul but a combination of the body, the senses, the ego (the organism and the personality) and what Krishna terms as 'Daivam', a somewhat mysterious and difficult concept to analyze. Some interpret it as luck or ones fortune which may arise from actions of previous births - operating independently of oneself. The question arises whether 'Daivam' is part of Prakriti (nature) or a facet of the Universal essence. It is clearly part of nature. One may interpret this element of Prakriti as something providential. Upheavals, natural calamities and fortunate events beyond ones control become enjoined with our own natural and mental propensities to produce the final action.

Then Krishna returns to Arjun's immediate situation. He says that one whose actions are untainted with egoism and longing for fruits of actions, in performing his duty selflessly remains unbound by Karma. He implies that in engaging in battle with such an attitude and mind-set, even killing his kinsmen his actions will remain untainted and his Karma will not bind him. One is reminded of the soldier fighting for his country in a war. He does not become a murderer or criminal as his motives are for an impersonal cause.

Krishna dwells further on the subject of action. The three elements are knowledge, the action and the actor. The actor who is free of attachment, non-egoistic, firm and zestful, who does not fear failure, having knowledge that the imperishable essence is in all existence, undivided in the divided and whose actions are free of attachment, without love or hate is pre-eminent. Such a person knows right from wrong.

The actor who is passionate and desirous of results, greedy, cruel and impure, moved by joy and sorrow, who has no belief in the ubiquitous presence of the Universal Essence in the phenomenal world and who acts with egoism and uses a lot of effort is the dynamic sort (Rajasik). Such a person does not know right from wrong.

The actor who is unsteady, vulgar, stubborn, deceitful, malicious, indolent, and procrastinating who believes without reason in a single idea which does not approximate to the truth and who acts whimsically from delusion, uncaring for consequences, and without heeding the limits of his abilities is an ignoramus (Tamasik). Such a person believes wrong to be right and vice versa. He has a perverted intellect.

The Gita in this last chapter also makes mention of the four castes.

There is a lot of controversy over what is meant here. Some hold that this cannot be interpreted as an endorsement of the rigid caste system into which this categorization degenerated and which produced its own evils of discrimination and inequity. They hold that the categories are a broad archetypal definition of occupations. What is meant is that a person with certain qualities is by his inner nature (Svabhava) Brahmin or Kshatriya etc. Even if this view were to be disputed in favour of the classical model of a hereditary caste system, one cannot but observe that when the scriptures appeared first it would be in a classical age or pre history when the concept was universally accepted and therefore the references are relevant to that age.

The ideal qualities of a Brahmin or order of wise sages and gurus and the priestly order are serenity, self restraint, austerity, purity, forgiveness, uprightness, knowledge, scientific curiosity and belief in a hereafter. This is said to be their inner nature (Svabhava). The qualities defining a Kshatriya, the martial class, are heroism, vigour, firmness, resourcefulness, bravery, generosity and lordliness. The Vaisyas are those whose occupation includes agriculture, cattle rearing and trade. The Sudras are those whose profession is service and labour.

There is no bar to enlightenment for any and as already mentioned in several chapters of the Gita, the divine essence is present without distinction in every being, irrespective of caste, profession and gender and the wise man is declared to be that person who knows this fact. The wise man is also expected to know that though the world appears divided, there is a unity that binds all beings. The person who is unaware of this is an ignoramus. The same rule applies to all, no matter how high or low, namely that one must perform ones duty to perfection and without regard to the fruit and whoever fails in this will meet his Karmic fate, be he a High priest, King of Kings or a humble labourer.

The Gita goes on to say:

"Better is ones own innate activity, though imperfect than the activity of another well performed." Thus the one trained to be a physician, were he to engage in trade, this would amount to waste of resources. This of course is a contentious issue and open to argument.

Then again the Gita asserts:

"One should not abandon ....the duty to which one is born, though it is attended by misfortune for all undertakings are enveloped by misfortune, as fire by smoke." This can be interpreted in several ways. What I believe is meant here is that one should not turn ones back to ones origins and abandon the responsibilities towards family to gain an easy way out. For instance if one happens to be the eldest of many siblings and the parents pass away one has to assume responsibility for them rather than abandoning them to destitution while fending for oneself. Obliquely this also castigates Arjun for wanting to turn away from confronting his own situation and doing his duty.

In conclusion Krishna tells Arjun that if he continues to be possessed by his ego and maintain that he will not fight, such a resolve would be in vain because his nature would impel him to fight. He however asks him to reflect on the matter fully and then act as he chooses. He asks him whether he has listened with an attentive mind and whether his delusion has ended. He then finally advises him to renounce all and take refuge in Him alone which would liberate him from all sins.

At long last a pensive Arjun replies that his delusion is destroyed and through Krishna's grace he has regained his senses. He asserts that he is free from doubt and that he will act according to Krishna's advice. The Great war of the Mahabharat epic then begins at Kurukshetra (in modern day Haryana state - now a place of pilgrimage) in which the forces of evil are routed.

Sanjay the clairvoyant narrator of the dialogue taking place on the battle field addresses the blind king Dhritarastra, the leader of the opposing Kauravas in his palace thus:

"O king, as I recall again and again this wonderful and holy dialogue between Krishna and Arjun, I rejoice again and again." "Wherever Krishna the lord of Yoga is, wherever Partha the wielder of the bow is, there are prosperity, victory and sound policy; such is my conviction."

Indeed, wherever circumstances play havoc with ones discrimination, there will be an inner voice, that of one's own charioteer, to guide one on to the path of rightful action.

MOKSHA SANYAS YOGA
(Excerpts)

The Blessed Lord said:

Some sages declare that all actions should be renounced as evil, while others say that sacrifice, almsgiving and austerity should not be renounced.
CH 18.3

Acts of sacrifice, almsgiving and austerity should not be given up; sacrifice, almsgiving and austerity are purifying to the wise.
CH 18.5

But even these actions should be performed relinquishing attachment and all thought of reward, O Partha, this is my certain and best belief.
CH 18.6

The abandonment of any obligatory duty is not right; such abandonment out of delusion is Tamasik.
CH 18.7

To renounce a duty out of fear of its difficulty or painfulness is a Rajasik renunciation and attracts no reward.
CH 18.8

Whatever obligatory work is done, O Arjun, only because it ought to be done, without attachment and abandoning thought of reward, that abandonment is Sattvik.
CH 18.9

It is indeed impossible for an embodied being to renounce action entirely. But he who renounces the fruit of action is regarded as one who has renounced.
CH 18.11

The body, the agent (ego), the various senses, the different functions and fifth Daivam (fortune/ providence)

Whatever actions a man performs with his body, speech or mind, whether right or wrong - these five are its cause.
CH 18.14 / 15

That being so, he who in imperfect understanding looks upon the Self as the agent - he does not see at all.
CH 18.16

The knowledge by which the one Imperishable Being is seen in all existence, undivided in the divided, know that that knowledge is Sattvik.

But that knowledge by which one sees in all beings manifold entities of different kinds varying from one another - know that that knowledge is Rajasik.

And the knowledge by which one believes that a single life is all there is, which with its unreasoning and trivial view sees not the cause, or the eternal reality, that knowledge is Tamsik.
CH 18.20 / 21 / 22

Serenity, self-restraint, austerity, purity, forgiveness and also uprightness, knowledge, discernment, belief in God - these are the duties of the Brahmans, born of their own nature.
CH 18.42

Bravery, vigour, firmness, skill and not fleeing from battle, generosity and royal demeanour are the mark of Kshatriyas born of their own nature.
CH 18.43

Agriculture, cattle rearing and trade are the duties of the Vaishyas, born of their own nature; and action consisting of service is the duty of the Sudras, born of their own nature.
CH 18.44

Better is one's own duty, though imperfect, than the duty of another well performed. He who does the duty ordained by his own nature incurs no sin.
CH 18.47

One should not abandon, O Kaunteya, the duty to which one is born, though it be imperfect, for all undertakings have imperfections even as fire is attended by smoke.
CH 18.48

If filled with egoism, you think "I will not fight", vain is this, your resolve; your nature will compel you.
CH 18.59

The Lord dwells in the heart of all beings, O Arjuna, and by his Maya causes all beings to revolve as though mounted on a machine.
CH 18.61

Seek refuge in Him alone with all your heart, O Bharata. By His grace you will gain supreme peace and the Eternal Abode.
CH 18.62

Thus has wisdom more profound than all profundities been declared to you by Me. Reflect upon it fully and act as you choose.
CH 18.63

He who with supreme devotion to Me will declare this immensely profound philosophy to My devotees, shall doubtless come to Me alone.
CH 18.68

And he who will study this sacred dialogue of ours, by him I shall have been worshipped through the path of knowledge; such is my conviction.
CH 18.70

Has this been heard by you, O Partha, with an attentive mind? Has the delusion of ignorance been destroyed, O Dhananjaya?
CH 18.72

Arjun said:

My delusion is destroyed. I have regained my understanding through Your grace, O Achyuta[37]. I am firm; I am free of doubt. I shall act according to Your word.
CH 18.73

---

37 Imperishable - Krishna.

Sanjay said:
O king, as I recall again and again this wonderful and holy dialogue between Keshava and Arjun I rejoice again and again.
CH 18.76

Wherever Krishna is, the Lord of Yoga, wherever Partha is, the archer, there I know are prosperity, victory, happiness and sound policy; such is my conviction.
CH 18.78

MAJOR THEMES WITH TEXTUAL REFERENCES

A. THE SOUL AND ITS LIBERATION

1. The Actionless Atma

The Atma is action less and therefore not tainted by the Karmas of several lifetimes. Neither the Atma nor Prabuh (God) are agents of action. It is the Gunas of Prakriti (nature and the traits of the individual) that are the agents of action.

Textual Referernces:

A yogi centred in the Self should think, 'I do nothing at all'- though seeing, hearing, touching, smelling, tasting, walking, sleeping, breathing, speaking, emptying, holding, opening and closing his eyes - firm in the thought that it is only the senses that are busy with sense objects.
CH 5.8 / 9

Having mentally renounced all actions, the self-disciplined indweller rests happily in the city of nine gates, neither acting nor causing action.
CH 5.13

The Lord does not create agency or actions for the world; He does not create fruitful consequences of action; Nature does all this.
CH 5.14

He truly sees, who sees that all actions are done by Prakriti alone and the Atma is action less.
CH 13.29

Having no beginning and possessing no Gunas, the Supreme Self, imperishable, though dwelling in the body, O Kaunteya, neither acts nor is tainted.
CH 13.31

When the beholder perceives that there is no agent of action other than the Gunas and knows Him who is higher than the Gunas, he enters into My Being.
CH 14.19

The body, the agent (ego), the various senses, the different functions and fifth Daivam (fortune/providence)

Whatever actions a man performs with his body, speech or mind, whether right or wrong - these five are its cause.
CH 18.14 / 15

That being so, he who in imperfect understanding looks upon the Self as the agent - he does not see at all.
CH 18.16

2. Embodiment and Liberation of The Atma

The Atma gets embodied on account of the play of Gunas (natural traits and forces) and remains fettered for numerous births. At death the subtle body carries forward the impressions and Karmic effects (Sanskaras) to a new birth. The gross and subtle body finally evolve to an enlightened state wherein the perfection of the Atma is mirrored by the gross and subtle body leading to the dissolution of Karmic effects. Then the Atma gets released from the physical bondage of rebirth, merging again with the Paramatma, the Super Soul or Universal Essence of God, Brahman.

Textual Referernces:

I am the Self, O Gudakesh, seated in the hearts of all beings, I am the beginning, the middle and also the end of all beings.
CH 10.20

An eternal portion of Myself having become the eternal soul in the living world, draws to itself Nature's five senses and the mind.
CH 15.7

Presiding over hearing, sight, touch, taste, smell, and mind, he experiences sense objects.
CH 15. 9

Sattva, Rajas, Tamas - these Gunas, O mighty-armed, born of Prakriti, bind the indestructible embodied one fast in the body.
CH 14.5

Of these, Sattva, being luminous and untroubled, binds by creating attachment to happiness and attachment to knowledge, O sinless one.
CH 14.6

Know Rajas to be of the nature of passion, the source of yearning and attachment; it fetters, O Kaunteya, the embodied one by attachment to action.
CH 14.7

But know Tamas to be born of ignorance, deluding all embodied beings; it fetters, O Bharata, by heedlessness, indolence and sleep.
CH 14.8

When this Sovereign-Soul which has been in the body, leaves, he takes these along, as the wind carries the scent from their sources.
CH 15.8

As the indweller in the body experiences childhood, youth and old age in the body, he also passes on to another body. The serene one is not affected thereby.
CH 2.13

As a man casting off worn out garments puts on new ones, so the embodied one, casting off worn out bodies enters into others that are new.
CH 2.22

The embodied one having crossed over these three Gunas out of which the body is evolved, is freed from birth, death, decay and pain and attains to immortality.
CH 14.20

He, O Pandava, who hates not light, activity and delusion, when present, nor craves for them when absent;

He who as one sitting unconcerned, is not shaken by the Gunas, who stands unaffected, knowing it is but the Gunas that move;
CH 14.22 / 23

Balanced in pleasure and pain, self-possessed, viewing a clod of earth, a stone and gold alike; the same towards the agreeable and the disagreeable, firm, the same in censure and praise;

The same in honour and dishonour, the same to friend and foe, renouncing all undertakings - he is said to have risen above the Gunas.
CH 14.24 / 25

3. Svabhava and Nishkam Karma

The ideal of life is to get to know ones true nature, Svabhava, which is the perfection of the indwelling Atma (Soul) an extension of Paramatma (Super-Soul), the Universal Essence, Brahman. The goal therefore is to recognize and access the divinity within. This is achieved through prayer, contemplation and meditation, but above all through dispassionate and altruistic action, Nishkam Karma. This mainly consists in performing action sincerely without obsessing about results and rewards. When this is perfected, Karmic effects dissolve and do not attach to the subtle body; enlightenment dawns as the Atma shines out, unveiled so to speak. The physical personality now fully matches the perfection of the Atma within having finally accessed it. Then there is no rebirth as the last gross body and final subtle body dissolves, releasing the Atma which merges with Brahman.

Textual Referernces:

You only have a right to your actions no claim to the fruits thereof; do not be moved by the fruits of action; nor be inclined to inaction.
CH 2.47

Motivated action is, O Dhananjaya , far inferior to that performed with equanimity of mind; take refuge in the evenness of the mind; wretched are the result seekers.
CH 2.49

The wise, imbued with evenness of mind, renouncing the fruits of their actions, freed from the fetters of births, verily go to the stainless state
CH 2.51

As the unenlightened act from attachment to action, O Bharata, so should the enlightened act without attachment, desirous of guiding the multitude.
CH 3.25

When one has renounced all desire for fruits of action and no longer clings to objects of the senses, then alone one is said to have attained to Yoga.
CH 6.4

Better indeed is knowledge than ritual practice; better than knowledge is meditation; better than meditation is the surrender of the fruits of action; peace immediately follows renunciation.
CH 12.12

If the embodied one faces dissolution when Sattva is predominant, then he goes to the pure world of the most exalted knowers.
CH 14.14

Facing dissolution in Rajas, he is born among those attached to action; and dying in Tamas, he is born in the wombs of the deluded.
CH 14.15

The yogi, abandoning attachment, performs action only with the body, the mind, the intellect and the senses, for the purification of the soul.
CH 5.11

Balanced in pleasure and pain, self-possessed, viewing a clod of earth, a stone and gold alike; the same towards the agreeable and the disagreeable, firm, the same in censure and praise;

The same in honour and dishonour, the same to friend and foe, renouncing all undertakings - he is said to have risen above the Gunas.

CH 14.24 / 25

The embodied one having crossed over these three Gunas out of which the body is evolved, is freed from birth, death, decay and pain and attains to immortality.

CH 14.20

4. Ego, the False Identity

The personality arising from the combination of Gunas forming the gross body in the current incarnation is sustained and driven by the false identity, the ego, which impels hedonistic action producing Karmic consequences. The ego gives rise to desire, lust and wrath, dominating the senses, the mind and the intellect and veiling the wisdom of the Atma which is the indweller and true identity.

Textual Referernces:

Given over to egoism, power, pride, desire and wrath, these malicious people hate Me dwelling in their own bodies and those of others.

CH 16.18

That man attains peace who lives devoid of longing, free from desires and without the feeling of 'I' and 'mine'.

CH 2.71

This, O Partha, is the state of abiding in Brahman, of absolute truth. Attaining this, none is deluded; if even only at his last hours he dwells in it he attains to oneness in Brahman.

CH 2. 72

5. Limitless Opportunities for Evolution

There are unlimited opportunities for evolution towards enlightenment. There is no permanent condemnation of any individual as evil or incorrigible. Rebirth provides a progression of opportunities. Even a sinner can become a saint and those who have failed to achieve perfection are provided suitable opportunities in the next life.

There are none who are hateful or dear, all are the same in His eyes on the evolutionary path to enlightenment. Indeed enlightenment is possible for everyone irrespective of caste creed or gender.

Textual Referernces:

What of the man possessed of faith but lacking self-control, whose mind deviates from Yoga, what end does he meet with, O Krishna, having failed to attain perfection in Yoga?
CH 6.37

The Blessed Lord said:

O Partha, Neither in this world nor in the next is there destruction for him; for, the doer of good, O my son, Never comes to grief.
CH 6.40

Having attained to the worlds of the righteous and having lived there countless years, he who falls from Yoga is reborn in the house of the pure and prosperous.
CH 6.41

There he regains the knowledge acquired in his former body and he strives more than before for perfection, O joy of Kurus.
CH 6.43

Even if a man of the most sinful conduct worships Me with undeviating devotion, he must be reckoned as righteous, for he has rightly resolved.
CH 9.30

Soon he becomes a man of righteousness and obtains lasting peace. O son of Kunti, know for certain that My devotee never comes to harm.
CH 9.31

I am the same to all beings; to Me there is none hateful, none dear. But those who worship Me with devotion, they are in Me and I also am in them.
CH 9.29

For those who take refuge in Me, O Partha, though they be of inferior birth - women, merchants, farmers and slaves - even they attain the Supreme Goal.
Ch 9.32

6. Obligatory Duty

Performance of obligatory duty dispassionately is a primary goal of life, leading to evolution of the personality in the current incarnation and eventually to enlightenment in later incarnations if the pace of evolution is consistently sustained. This consists in discharging responsibility towards family, community and the world at large, being diligent, dexterous and industrious and righteous, fighting for and supporting what is right. Abdication and abandonment of responsibility through disinclination, fear or mistaken and premature asceticism and reclusion is deemed false renunciation which does not lead to salvation. Renunciation means renouncing fruits of action by engaging in unattached action and not the renunciation of ones obligatory duty. Even God is constantly engaged in discharging his responsibility and acting to sustain his creation setting an example for the performance of obligatory duty.

Textual Referernces:

Engage yourself in obligatory work; for action is superior to inaction, and if inactive, even the mere maintenance of your body would not be possible.
CH 3.8

Therefore, constantly perform your obligatory duty without attachment; for, by doing duty without attachment man verily obtains the Supreme.
CH 3.19

None can ever remain really actionless even for a moment; for everyone is helplessly driven to action by the Gunas, born of Prakriti.
CH 3.5

That deluded man is called a hypocrite who sits controlling the organs of action, but dwelling in his mind on the objects of the senses.
CH 3.6

Renunciation is hard to attain without the yoga of action; the man of meditation, purified by the yoga of action soon attains to the enlightened state.
CH 5.6

The abandonment of any obligatory duty is not right; such abandonment out of delusion is Tamasik.
CH 18.7

It is indeed impossible for an embodied being to renounce action entirely. But he who renounces the fruit of action is regarded as one who has renounced.
CH 18.11

One should not abandon, O Kaunteya, the duty to which one is born, though it be imperfect, for all undertakings have imperfections even as fire is attended by smoke.
CH 18.48

There is nought in the three worlds, O Partha, that has not been done by me, nor anything unattained that might be attained; still I engage in action.
CH 3.22

If ever I did not engage in work relentless, O Partha, men would in every respect follow my path.
CH 3. 23

These worlds would perish if I did not do action; I should be the cause of confusion of species and I should destroy these beings.
CH 3.24

B. THE NATURE OF GOD AND WORSHIP

1. Divinity is Ubquitous-Inculcating Same-Sightedness

Externally divinity is ubiquitous, in every atom of creation and internally it is situated within as the indweller, the Atma. Recognition of this leads to an attitude of Sam Darshinah or same-sightedness, the understanding that every individual and every facet of creation is imbued with innate divinity. Therefore every individual, creature and aspect of creation has to be honoured, and treated with respect and consideration. One should therefore apply the same norms to others which one wishes for oneself. While our world looks diverse, in essence it is one grand unity in the apparent diversity.

Textual Referernces:

He sees, who sees the Supreme Lord, remaining the same in all beings, the imperishable in the perishable.
CH 13.27

The knowledge by which the one Imperishable Being is seen in all existence, undivided in the divided, know that that knowledge is Sattvik.

But that knowledge by which one sees in all beings manifold entities of different kinds varying from one another - know that that knowledge is Rajasik.

And the knowledge by which one believes that a single life is all there is, which with its unreasoning and trivial view sees not the cause, or the eternal reality, that knowledge is Tamsik.
CH 18.20 / 21 / 22

Dedicated to the path of action with a purified mind, self disciplined and with the senses subdued one who recognizes his Self as the Self in all beings, though acting remains untainted.
CH 5.7

Men of Self-knowledge see the Eternal equally in a wise and courteous Brahman, a cow, an elephant, a dog and an outcast.
CH 5.18

They rise above this transitory existence whose minds abide in this sense of equality, for Brahman is unblemished and the same in all; such people become established in Brahman.
CH 5.19

His mind being harmonized by Yoga, he sees himself in all beings and all beings in himself; he sees the same in all.
CH 6.29

He who sees Me everywhere and sees all in Me, he never becomes lost to Me, nor do I become lost to him.
CH 6.30

He who, established in oneness, worships Me abiding in all beings, that Yogi lives in Me, wheresoever he may abide.
CH 6.31

That Yogi, O Arjun, is regarded as the supreme, who judges pleasure and pain everywhere by the same standard as he applies to himself.
CH 6.32

Behold now, O Gudakesh, the whole universe of the moving and the unmoving joined together as one in my body and whatever else you desire to see.
CH 11.7

There in the body of the God of gods, Pandava then beheld the whole universe, in its manifold diversity, drawn together into one.
CH 11.13

With hands and feet everywhere, with eyes and hands and mouths everywhere, with ears everywhere - He exists enveloping all.

Shining through the functions of the senses, yet without the senses; Unattached yet sustaining all; devoid of Gunas, yet He experiences them.

Without and within all beings; the unmoving and also the moving; because of His subtlety He is incomprehensible; He is far and near.
CH 13.13 / 14 / 15

He is undivided and yet He seems divided in beings. He is to be known as the supporter of beings. He devours and He generates.
CH 13.16

2. An Intimate God

The Hindu concept of God is not just of an omnipotent, omniscient heavenly being rather that of an intimate and familiar even friendly and companionable personage; not merely a father figure, but a friend and even a beloved. As an Avatar He becomes a manifestation of the Absolute Unmanifest (Brahman) arriving periodically on the material plane to redress and reform his atrophying creation. Krishna is an Avatar and Arjun is his friend. When he is shown His cosmic form he apologizes for treating him as a friend in very touching verses. The Hindu concept of God has necessarily to be intimate for the simple reason that the Self or Atma residing within is itself a projection of Brahman. There is no need to seek him in the distant heavens when in fact He resides in ones innermost core.

Textual Referernces:

I am the father of this world, the mother, the sustainer and the grandsire; I am the object of knowledge, the purifier, the syllable Om and the three Vedas.
CH 9.17

I am the goal, the supporter, the Lord, the Witness, the abode, the shelter, the friend, the Origin, the dissolution, the foundation, the treasure house and the seed imperishable.
CH 9.18

Though I am unborn, imperishable and the Lord of beings, yet subjugating my Prakriti, I take birth by my own Maya.
CH 4.6

Whenever there is decay of virtue and rise of lawlessness, then I embody myself, O Bharata.
CH 4.7

For the protection of the good, for the destruction of the wicked and for the establishment of dharma I am born age after age.
CH 4.8

Whatever I have said from carelessness or love, addressing You as 'O Krishna, O Yadav, O friend', presumptuously, looking upon You merely as a friend, ignorant of this your greatness; In whatever way I may have shown disrespect in jest or at play, reposing, sitting or at meals, whether alone or in company - that I implore You, Immeasurable One, to forgive.
CH 11.41 / 42

Therefore, bowing down, prostrating my body, I implore You adorable Lord to forgive me. Bear with me, Lord as a father with his son, as a friend with his friend, as a lover with his beloved.
CH 11.44

3. Worshipping the Manifest and the Unmanifest

Worshipping the manifest godhead (Sagun Brahma) is given preference over worshipping the unmanifest godhead (Nirgun Brahma) because for an embodied being the worship of the unmanifest or formless is explained as being both difficult and troubling. The tenor of tolerance for all forms of worship is in clear evidence.
However, the worship of divinity with form in the shape of Krishna or the numerous gods of the Hindu pantheon have clear sanction without denying worship of the formless as equally legitimate if more difficult.

Textual Referernces:

Those who, fixing their minds on me, worship me with perpetual devotion, endowed with supreme faith - them do I consider most perfect in the Rule.
CH 12.2

But those who worship the Imperishable, the Indefinable, the Unmanifested, the Omnipresent, the Unthinkable, the Unchangable, the, Immovable, the Eternal; having restrained all their senses, even minded everywhere, rejoicing in the welfare of all beings - win to Me also.
CH 12.4

Greater is their difficulty whose minds are set on the Unmanifested, for the goal of the Unmanifested is very hard for the embodied to reach.
CH 12.5

4. Tolerance for Diverse Paths of Worship

A tolerant and inclusive approach towards diverse paths of worship is a recurring feature of the Gita. All paths of worship it is emphasized reach the same divine goal and are acceptable. God appears to the worshipper in the form he conceives. Whatever the form of worship God acknowledges the prayer.

Textual Referernces:

In whatever way men seek me, in the same way do I carry out their desires; men pursue my path, O Partha, in all ways.
CH 4.11

Whatever divine form any devotee with faith wishes to worship, that same faith in him I make unwavering.
CH 7.21

Endowed with that faith, he engages in the worship of that form and from it obtains his desires, which are actually being ordained by Me.
CH 7.22

But the fruit that accrues to those men of small intellect is finite. The worshippers of the gods go to the gods; My devotees come to Me.
CH 7.23

Yet others sacrifice with the Yagya of knowledge and worship Me in various ways as the one, as several or as diverse with many facets.
Ch 9.15

Even those devotees who, with faith, worship other gods, worship Me alone, O son of Kunti, by a contrary method.
CH 9.23

Sattvik men worship the gods; Rajsik, the demigods and demons; the others - the Tamsik men - the spirits of the dead and ghosts and nature spirits.
CH 17.4

Worshippers of the gods go to the gods; worshippers of the ancestors go to the ancestors; worshippers of the ghosts go to the ghosts; but those who worship Me come to Me.
CH 9.25

I am the same to all beings; to Me there is none hateful, none dear. But those who worship Me with devotion, they are in Me and I also am in them.
CH 9.29

5. Disciplined Spirituality Through Moderation

The Gita enjoins moderation in practice of austerities and spiritual disciplines and in conduct in general and does not appear to favour extreme penances. It holds disciplined spirituality superior to mere ritualism and unbounded austerities.

Textual Referernces:

Yoga is not possible for him who eats too much or for him who abstains too much from eating; it is not for him, O Arjun, who sleeps too much or too little.
CH 6.16

For him who is moderate in eating and recreation, temperate in his actions, who is regulated in sleep and wakefulness, Yoga becomes the destroyer of pain.
CH 6.17

By that very former practice he is led on in spite of himself. Even he who merely wishes to know of Yoga rises superior to the performer of mere rituals of worship.
CH 6.44

The Yogi is deemed superior to ascetics, superior to men of knowledge even; he is also superior to ritualists. Therefore be you a Yogi, O Arjun.
CH 6.46

Those men who practice grim mortifications not ordained by the scriptures, conceited and hypocritical, impelled by the force of lust and attachments, fools that they are, they torture their bodily organs and Me too, who dwells within the body - know that they are demonic in their resolve.
CH 17.5 / 6

That austerity which is practiced with a foolish obstinacy, with self-tortures or for the purpose of destroying another, is declared to be Tamasik.
CH 17.19

Whatever is sacrificed, given or performed and whatever austerity is practiced without faith, it is called Asat (false), O Partha, and is worthless both here and in the hereafter.
CH 17.28

INDEX

A

abandonment (tyag), 99, 100
abhyasa, 71
adhibhuta, 45, 46
adhidaiva, 45, 46
adhiyagya, 45, 46
Advaita, non-dualism, 30
adyatma, 45, 46
ahankara (ego), 29, 76
allegorical connotations, 3, 25
ansha, 83, 88
antaryami (indweller), 9, 23, 77
Arjun the hero, 15, 64
asat (false), 97
atma (self / soul), 8-10, 23, 38, 56;
embodiment of, 77-82, 83;
inconceivable, 32;
unthinkable, none knows it, 13;
quiescent and non acting, 28, 32, 79, 83, 86, 101, 105, 110;
reincarnation of, 83; liberation of, 84
uncontaminated by Karma, 10, 101
austerities, 95–98
avatar, 6, 22-25, 35, 38, 43, 49, 55, 56

B

Besant, Anne, 17
Bhakti movement, 31
Brahma, 16, 30, 46, 47, 66
Brahman, 41, 46, 57;
Gita's description of, 84
Brahmi, state of, 12

C

castes, caste system, 102, 104, 106
celestial eyes, divine sight (divyam chakshuhu), 61, 62
cosmic colossus (virat), 63, 64

D

Daivam, providence, 101, 105
Devas (divine beings, gods), 17, 51
dexterous, quality of a favourite devotee, 71
Dharma, 22, 26
Dhritarashtra, 3, 4
Divine Essence (Brahman), 29, 77, 84
dispassionate action, 27, 28; Krishna the role model for, 50
dogmatic Vedic orthodoxy, 9
Duryodhana, 3, 24
duty to which one is born, 103

E

egalitarian, egalitarianism, 29, 50
ego, 3, 12, 29, 41, 45, 76
embodied one (indweller, Self, soul), 13
empty Vedic ritualism, 37
enlightened bliss, 12
environmental consciousness, 36

G

gneyam, what ought to be known, 76

gross body, 9
gunas, 16, 17-19, 28, 76, 79, 81, 82, 85, 86 as agent of action, 83
gyan indriya, senses of knowledge, 76

H

higher nature (God's), 41, 43
humanitarian, 37

I

Ikshvaku, 22
indweller, 8, 10.13; indestructible, 8; non-acting, 32, 33; reincarnation of, 83
inner self, 28, 38, 41

J

jiva, jivatama, 9

K

kama, 41
Karma, not bound by, 23
karma indriya, organs of action, 76
Kaurava, 2, 3, 104
Krishna, childhood, adolescent, 24
Kurukshetra, 2, 24, 103

M

Mahabharat, 16, 25, 35, 104
Manu, 21
maya, 22, 26, 29
Maya Shakti, 22
moderation, moderate, 36, 38, 39
Monist, 30, 70

N

Nirgun Brahma, unmanifest godhead, 70, 71
Nishkam Karma, unattached action, 11, 28
Nirvana, 32

O

Obligatory duty, 100; God's, 17

P

Pandava, 2, 3, 24
Paramatma, 10, 46, 77, 87
Param Dham (Supreme Abode), 46
Partha, 12, 16, 64
Patanjali Yoga Darshan, 38
Prajapati, 16
prakriti, 16, 17, 19, 28, 41, 50, 75, 77, 78, 79, 81, 85, 101
Pranayam, 30, 38
Purush, 9, 46, 75-79
Purushottam, 88, 89

R

Ramayana, 25, 31, 92
Ravana, 92
Renunciation (sanyas), 27, 28, 100

S

Sagun Brahma, manifest godhead, 69, 70
sama darshinah, 28
same sightedness, 28, 36
Sanjay, clairvoyant narrator of Gïta's dialogues, 4, 104
sankalp, 37
Sankya, 16, 37
Sankya Karika, 37
sanyasi, 37, 38
sanskaras, 10
sex, 41

Srimad Bhagawat, 25
svabhava, ones true nature, 24, 46, 102

T

tolerance, 50, 69
Transcendental Monism, 29

U

undifferentiated action, supreme exzmple of, 17
unity in diversity, 29
Universal Consciousness, 29. 59, 60
Universal Essence, 10, 55, 59, 81
Universal Presence, 42

V

Vedas, 12
Vedantin, 30
Vedic thought, 35
Virat, 61, 64
Vivasvat, 22

Y

Yagya, 17, 37, 53

BOOKS OF RELATED INTEREST FROM NAB

APAD-DHARMA IN THE MAHABHARATA: How to Face Calamities at Personal, State and Global Levels—*Satya P. Agarwal*

"The present study poses an important, academic question: How could the Indian society have protected itself against external attacks during the pre-modern period?"

ISBN: 978-81-7822-361-2

GĪTĀ FOR SUCCESS IN MODERN LIFE: From Basement to Boardroom—*R.S. Garg*

This book discusses and explains the implications of certain parts of Bhagavad-Gītā insofar as they affect the daily life of a reasonably well-placed person. The text written in simple language is particularly aimed at the forever-busy and on the move folk.

ISBN: 978-81-7822-125-0

GĪTĀ FOR THE TWENTY-FIRST CENTURY: Bhagavad Gītā Universal Message

—*Satya P. Agarwal*

This version of Bhagavad-Gītā explains how the message of social service has been derived from this universal scripture.

ISBN: 978-81-7822-153-3

ŚRĪMAD BHAGAVAD GĪTĀ : Introduction, Sanskrit Text in Roman, English Translation including translation of every word

— *Kailash Nath Kalia*

Here is a rendering of *Śrīmad Bhagavad Gītā* into English. The main feature of this translation is that the Sanskrit text has also been given in the Roman script. This enables those readers who do not know Sanskrit to get a fairly correct idea of the spirit of the epic.

ISBN: 978-81-7822-306-3